FOR ORGANS, PIANOS & ELECTRONIC KEYBOARDS

56

American Folksongs & Spirituals

ISBN 0-634-01832-9

HAL•LEONARD®
CORPORATION
7777 W. BLUEMOUND RD. P.O. BOX 13819 MILWAUKEE, WI 53213

E-Z Play ® Today Music Notation © 1975 by HAL LEONARD CORPORATION

E-Z PLAY and EASY ELECTRONIC KEYBOARD MUSIC are registered trademarks of HAL LEONARD CORPORATION.

Visit Hal Leonard Online at
www.halleonard.com

American Folksongs & Spirituals

Contents

Folksongs

7 All the Pretty Little Horses

8 Animal Fair

10 Arkansas Traveler

9 Aura Lee

12 Blow the Candles Out

14 The Blue Tail Fly (Jimmy Crack Corn)

16 The Boll Weevil

18 Buffalo Gals (Won't You Come Out Tonight?)

20 Bury Me Not on the Lone Prairie

22 Cindy

24 (Oh, My Darling) Clementine

19 Cotton Eyed Joe

26 The Cruel War Is Raging

34 Down in the Valley

36 The Drunken Sailor

38 The Erie Canal

44 Frankie and Johnny

46 Git Along, Little Dogies

50 High Barbaree

52 Home on the Range

54 House of the Rising Sun

56 How Can I Keep from Singing

43 Hush, Little Baby

58 I've Been Working on the Railroad

64 John Henry

61 Li'l Liza Jane

80 Oh! Susanna

82 The Old Chisholm Trail

75 Old Joe Clark

84 On Top of Old Smoky

86 Once I Had a Sweetheart

88 Polly Wolly Doodle

92 The Red River Valley

94	She'll Be Comin' 'Round the Mountain
96	Shenandoah
98	Shoo Fly, Don't Bother Me
97	Shortnin' Bread
100	Simple Gifts
102	Skip to My Lou
114	Sourwood Mountain
118	Streets of Laredo
120	Sweet Betsy from Pike
126	There Is a Tavern in the Town
121	Turkey in the Straw
132	The Wabash Cannon Ball
138	When Johnny Comes Marching Home
135	When the Saints Go Marching In
140	Wondrous Love
142	Yankee Doodle

Spirituals

4	All My Trials
28	Deep River
30	Didn't My Lord Deliver Daniel?
40	Every Time I Feel the Spirit
48	He's Got the Whole World in His Hands
62	Jacob's Ladder
66	Joshua (Fit the Battle of Jericho)
68	Let Us Break Bread Together
70	The Lonesome Road
72	Never Said a Mumblin' Word
78	Nobody Knows the Trouble I've Seen
89	Rock-a-My Soul
103	Somebody's Knockin' at Your Door
106	Sometimes I Feel Like a Motherless Child
108	Soon Ah Will Be Done
111	Standin' in the Need of Prayer
116	Steal Away
122	Swing Low, Sweet Chariot
124	There Is a Balm in Gilead
128	This Little Light of Mine
136	Wayfaring Stranger
144	*Registration Guide*

All My Trials

Registration 1
Rhythm: Rock or Pops

African-American Spiritual

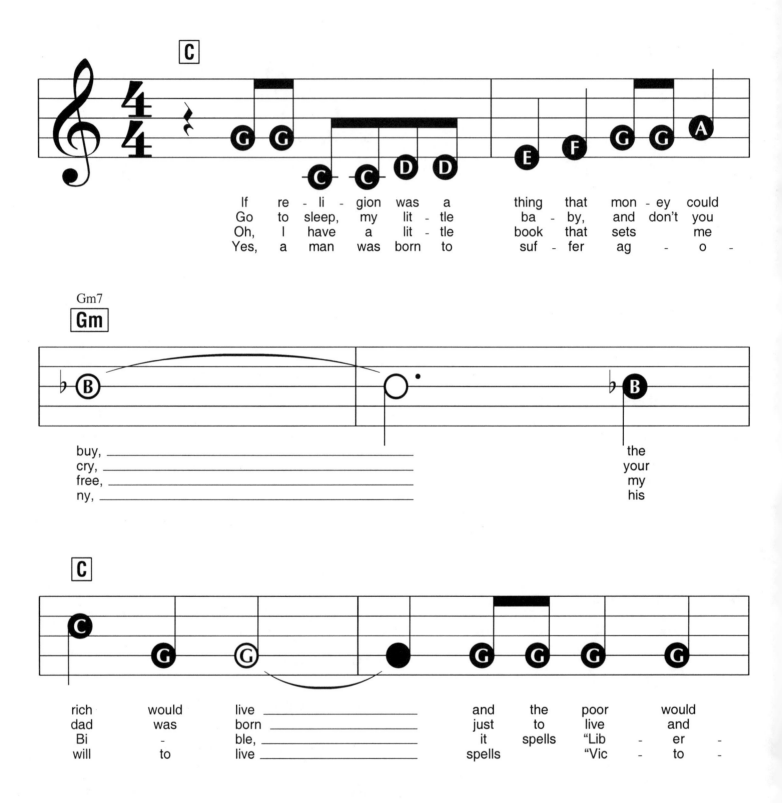

5

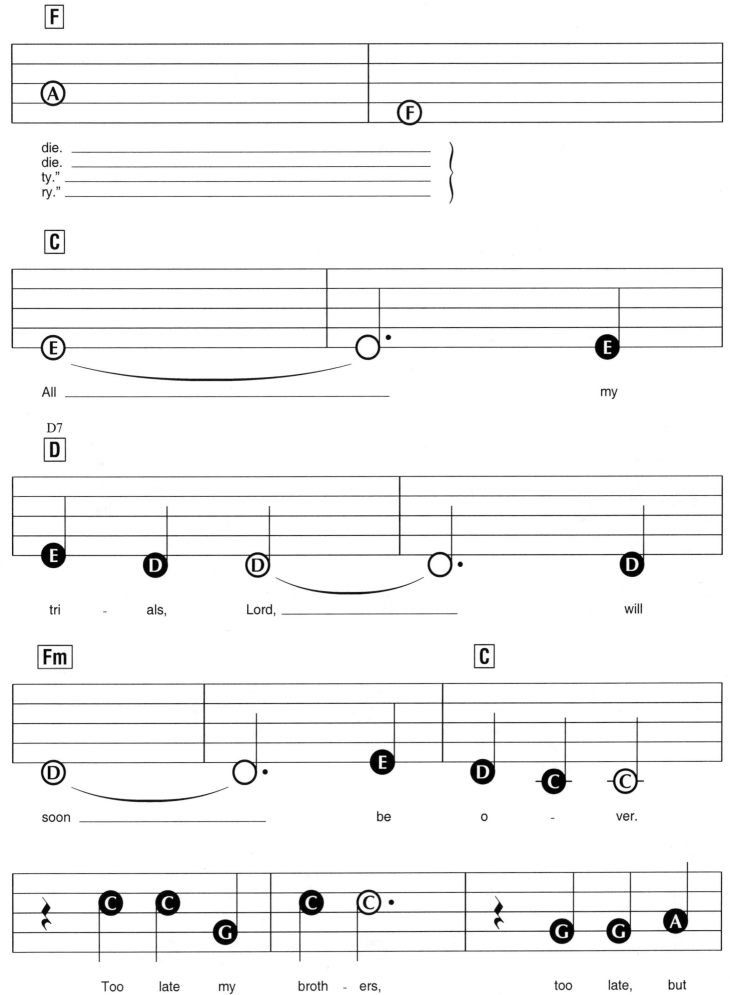

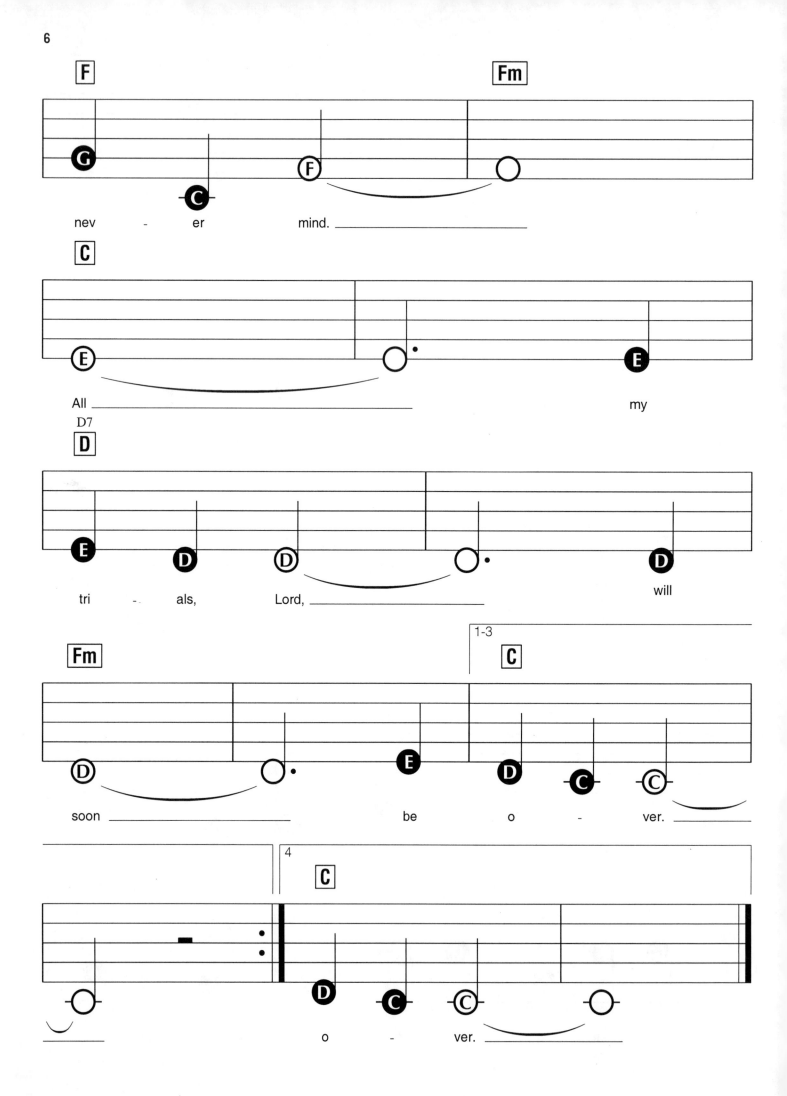

All the Pretty Little Horses

Registration 1
Rhythm: Fox Trot

Southeastern American Folksong

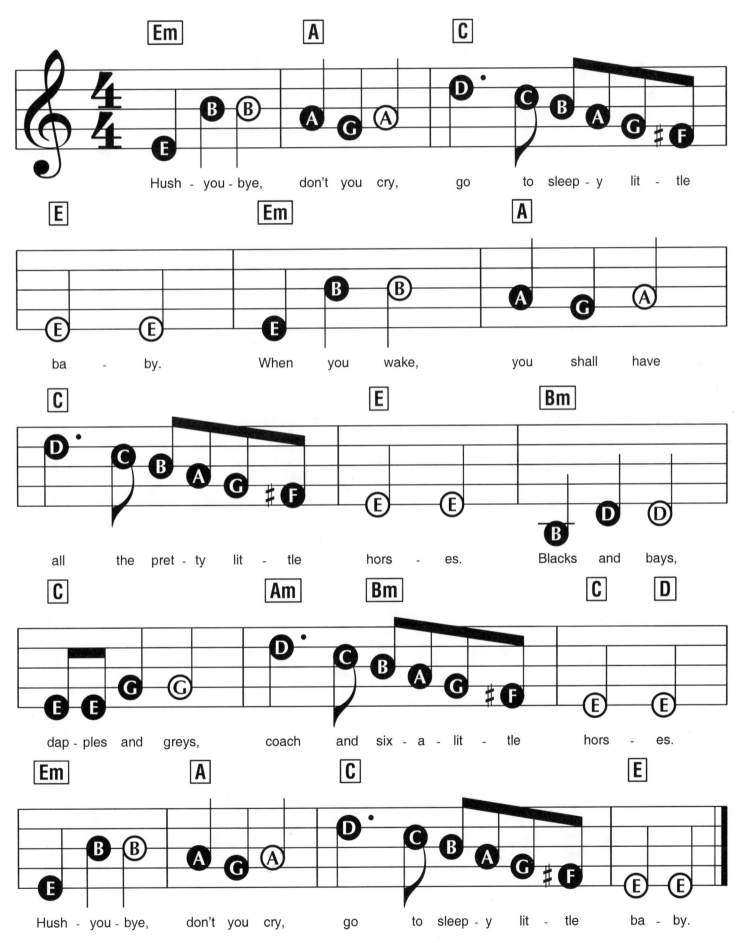

Animal Fair

Registration 4
Rhythm: 6/8 March

American Folksong

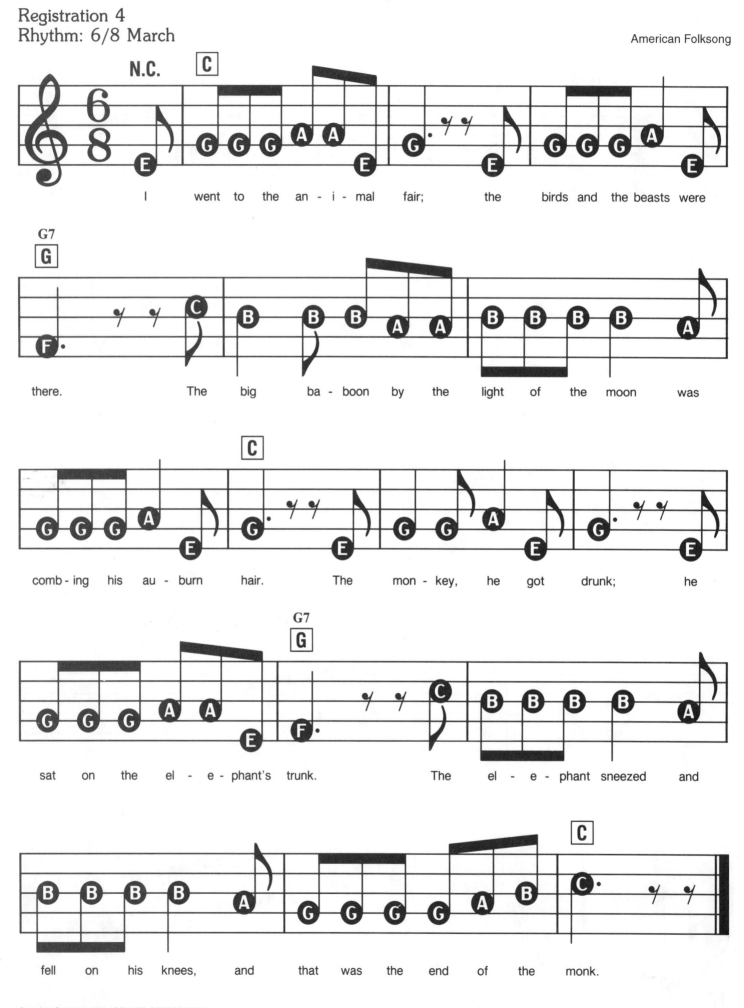

Aura Lee

Registration 3
Rhythm: Swing

Words by W.W. Fosdick
Music by George R. Poulton

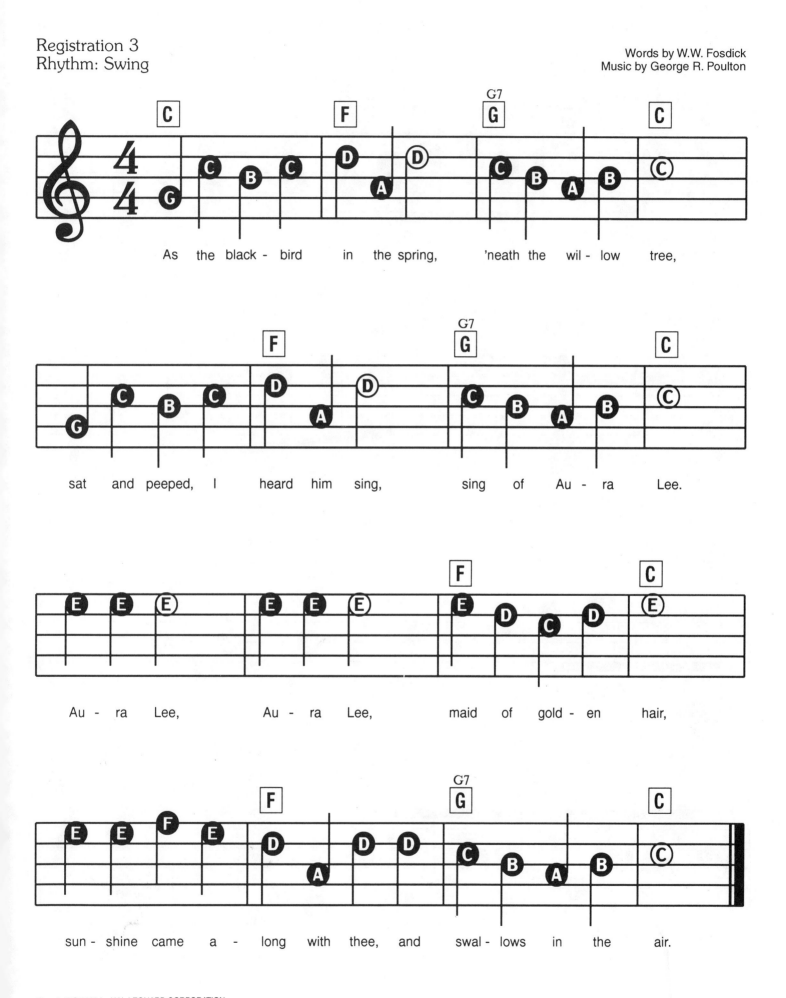

Arkansas Traveler

Registration 8
Rhythm: Country or Fox Trot

Southern American Folksong

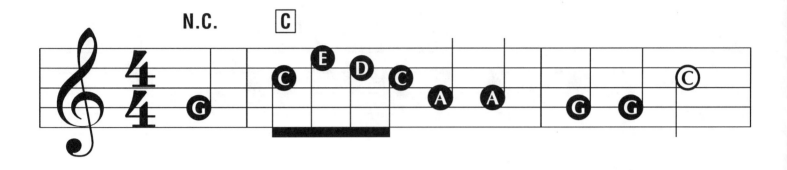

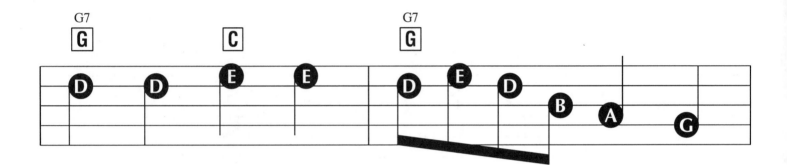

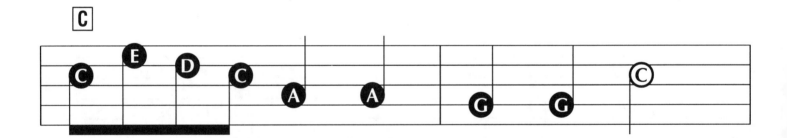

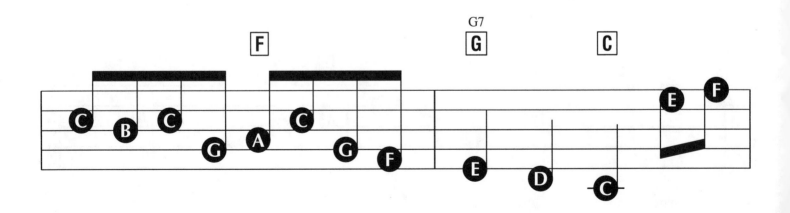

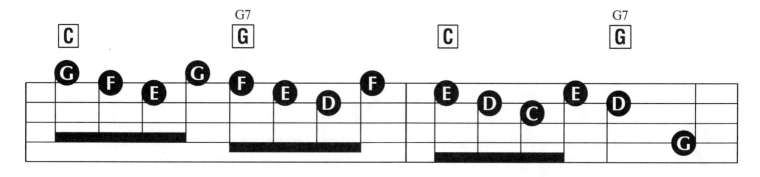

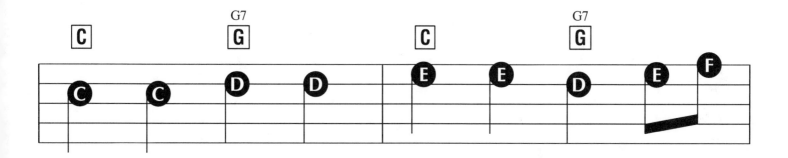

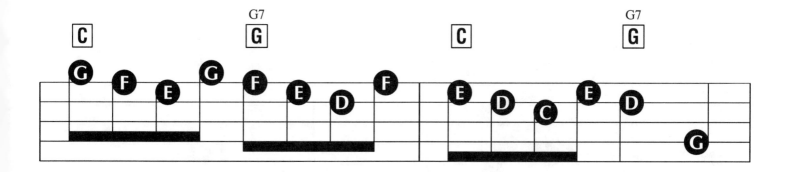

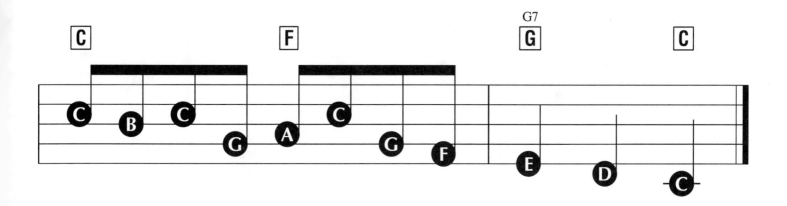

Blow the Candles Out

Registration 2
Rhythm: Fox Trot

American Folksong

1. When I was ap - pren - ticed in Lon - don, I
(2.) like your well be - hav - iour and
(3.) fa - ther, and your moth - er in
(4.) if you and prove suc - cess - ful, love, pray

went to see my dear. _____ The
thus I of - ten say, _____ I
yon - der room do lie, _____ A -
name it af - ter me, _____

can - dles were _____ all burn - ing, the
can - not rest _____ con - tent - ed whilst
hug - gin' one _____ an - oth - er, so
Keep it neat _____ and kiss it sweet, and

moon shone bright and clear. I knocked up - on her
you are far a - way. The roads they are so
why not you and I? A - hug - gin' one an -
daff it on your knee, When my three years are

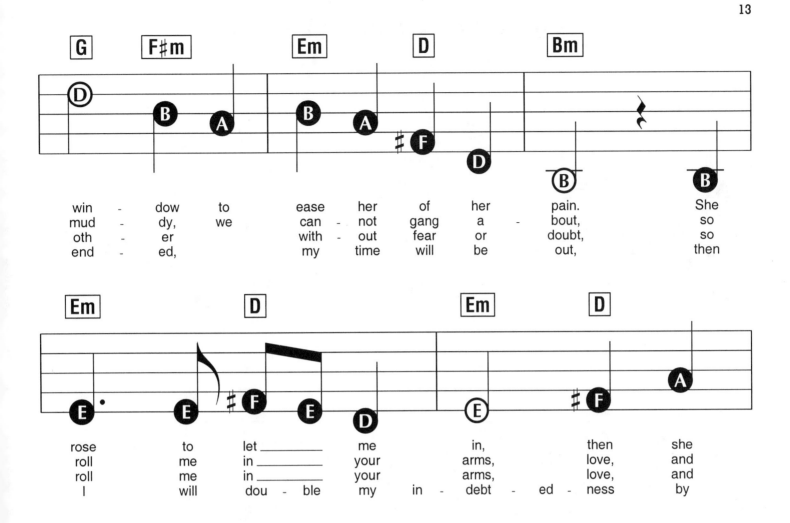

win - dow to ease her of her pain. She so
mud - dy, we can - not gang a - bout, so
oth - er with - out fear or doubt, so
end - ed, my time will be out, then

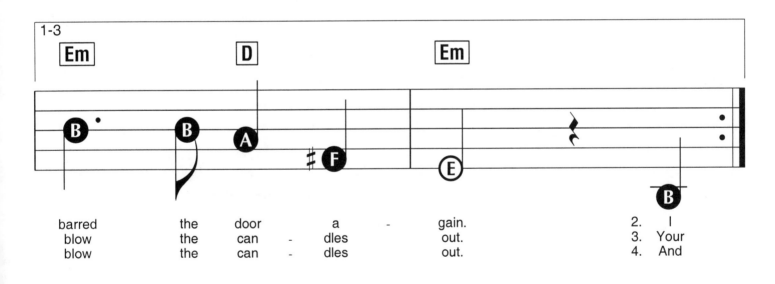

rose to let _____ me in, then she
roll me in _____ your arms, love, and
roll me in _____ your arms, love, and
I will dou - ble my in - debt - ed - ness by

1-3

barred the door a - gain. 2. I
blow the can - dles out. 3. Your
blow the can - dles out. 4. And

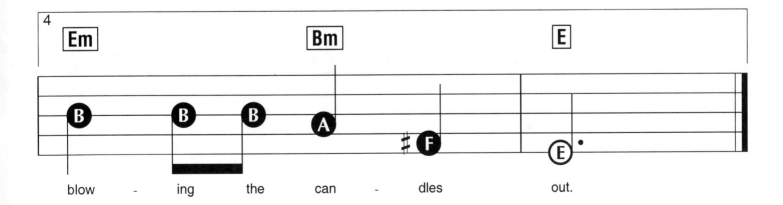

blow - ing the can - dles out.

The Blue Tail Fly
(Jimmy Crack Corn)

Registration 4
Rhythm: Fox Trot

Words and Music by
Daniel Decatur Emmett

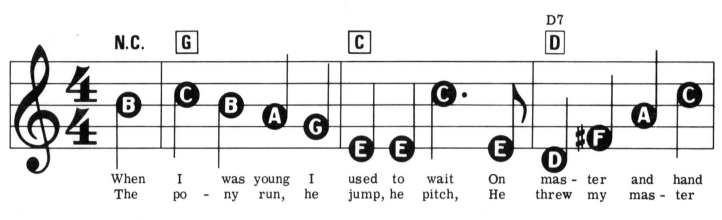

When I was young I used to wait, On mas - ter and hand
The po - ny run, he jump, he pitch, He threw my mas - ter

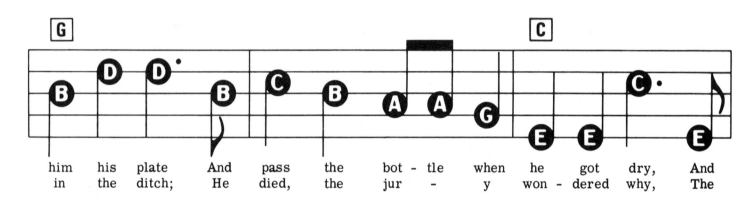

him his plate; And pass the bot - tle when he got dry, And
in the ditch; He died, the jur - y won - dered why, And The

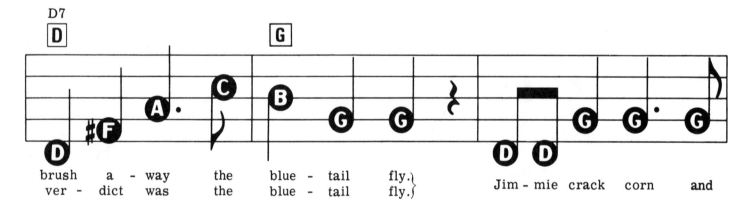

brush a - way the blue - tail fly.
ver - dict was the blue - tail fly. Jim - mie crack corn and

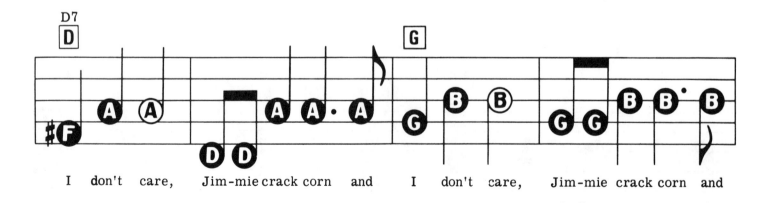

I don't care, Jim-mie crack corn and I don't care, Jim-mie crack corn and

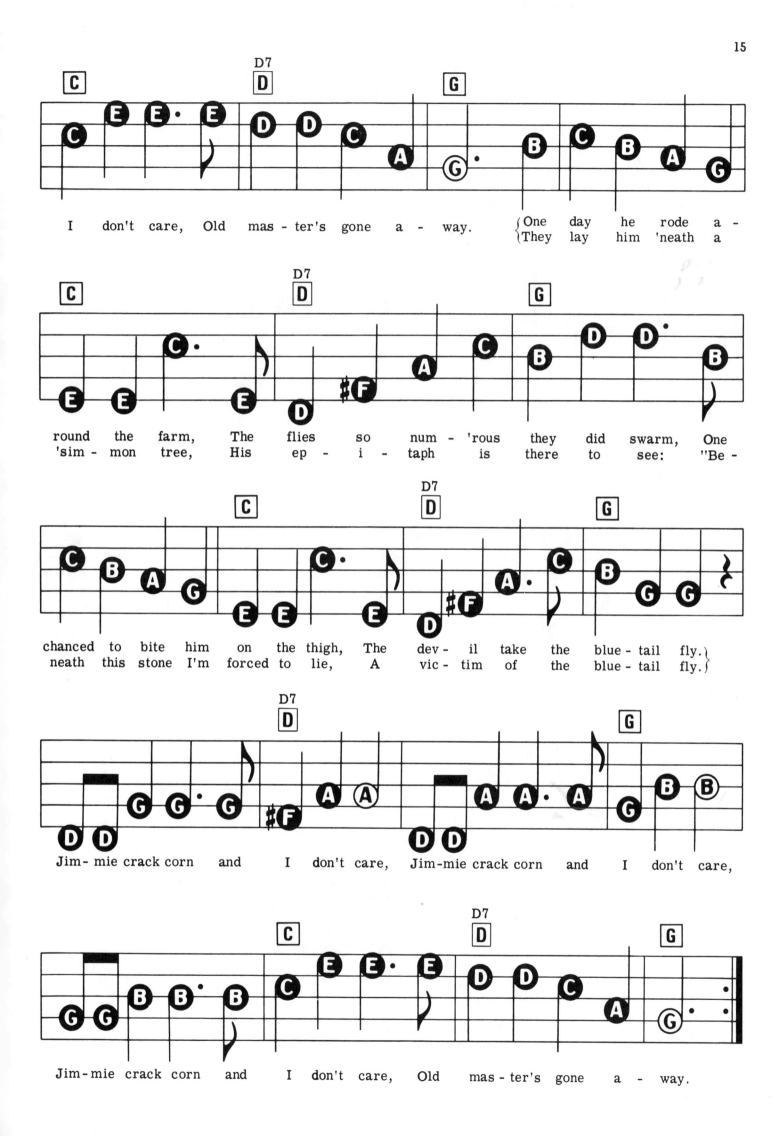

The Boll Weevil

Registration 3
Rhythm: Fox Trot

Texas Folksong

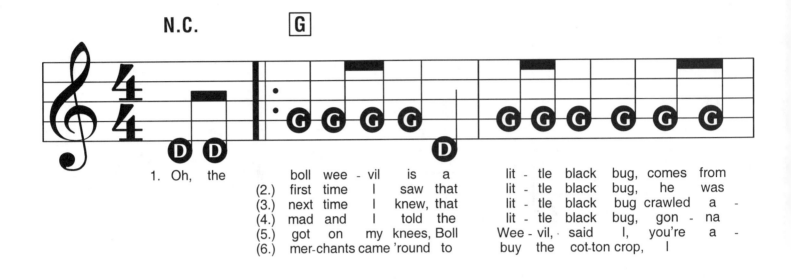

1. Oh, the boll wee - vil is a lit - tle black bug, comes from
(2.) first time I saw that lit - tle black bug, he was
(3.) next time I knew, that lit - tle black bug crawled a -
(4.) mad and I told the lit - tle black bug, gon - na
(5.) got on my knees, Boll Wee - vil, said I, you're a -
(6.) mer-chants came 'round to buy the cot-ton crop, I

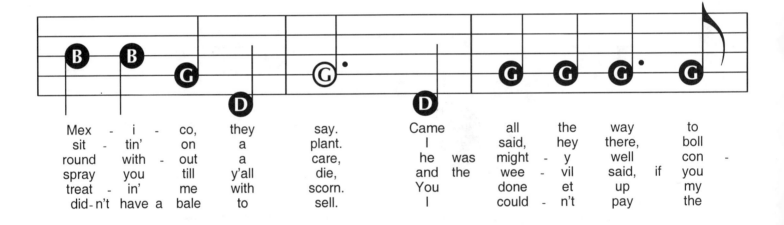

Mex - i - co, they say. Came all the way to
sit - tin' on a plant. I said, hey there, boll
round with - out a care, he was might - y well con -
spray you till y'all die, and the wee - vil said, if you
treat - in' me with scorn. You done et up my
did - n't have a bale to sell. I could - n't pay the

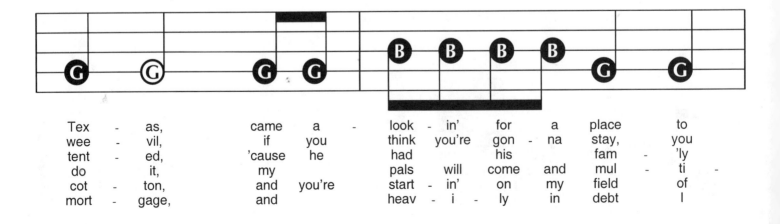

Tex - as, came a - look - in' for a place to
wee - vil, if you think you're gon - na stay, you
tent - ed, 'cause he had his fam - 'ly
do it, my pals will come and mul - ti -
cot - ton, and you're start - in' on my field of
mort - gage, and heav - i - ly in debt I

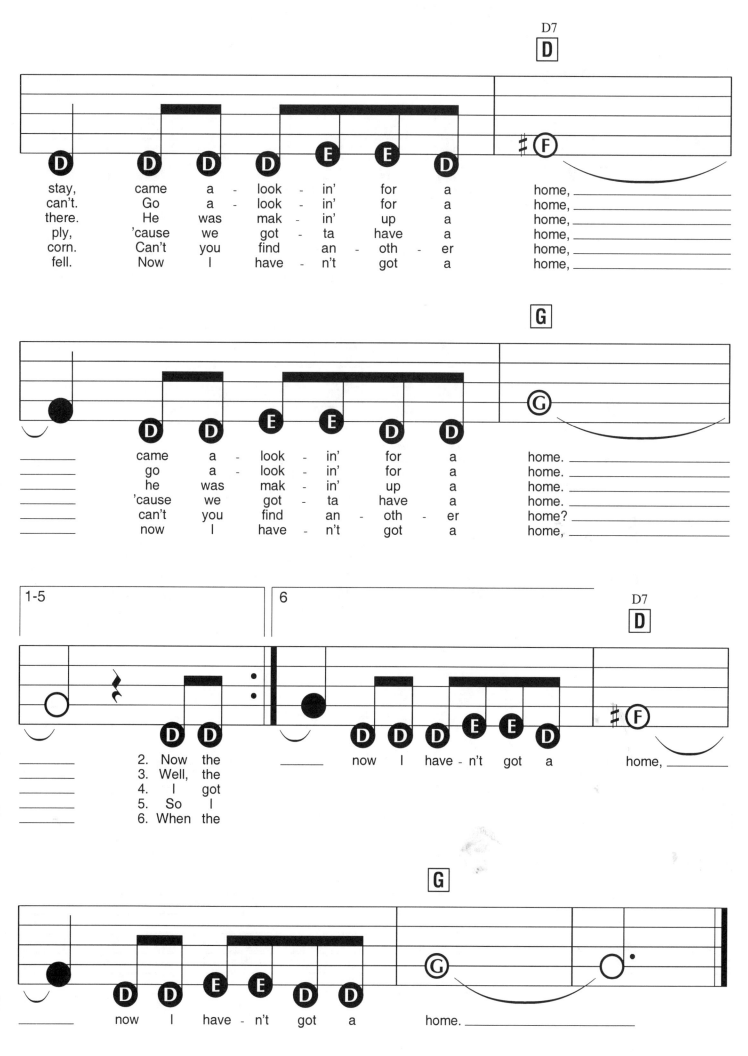

Buffalo Gals
(Won't You Come Out Tonight?)

Registration 10
Rhythm: Rock or 8 Beat

Words and Music by
Cool White (John Hodges)

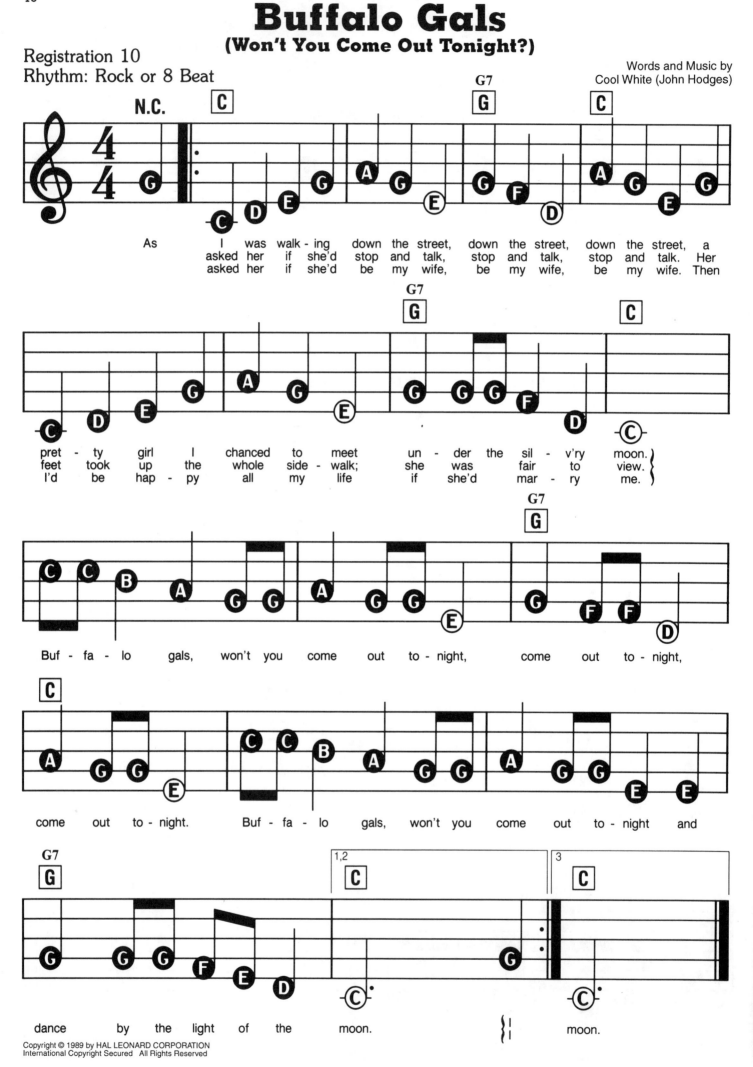

Cotton Eyed Joe

Registration 8
Rhythm: Country or Fox Trot

Tennessee Folksong

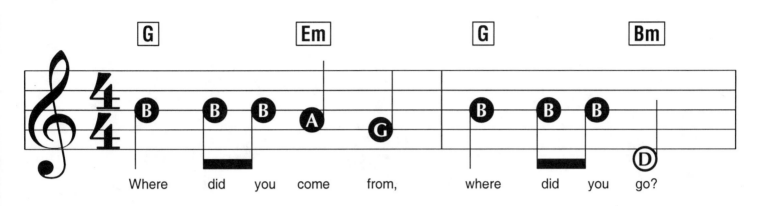

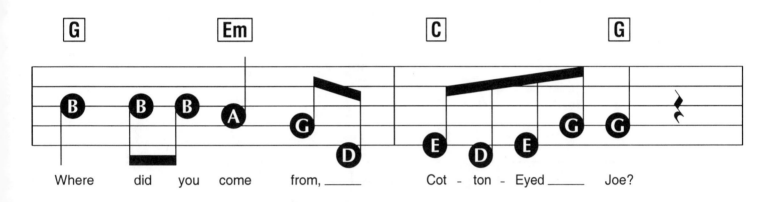

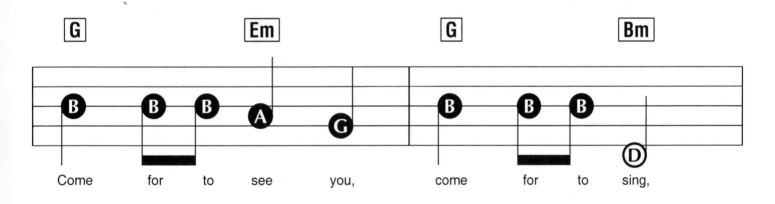

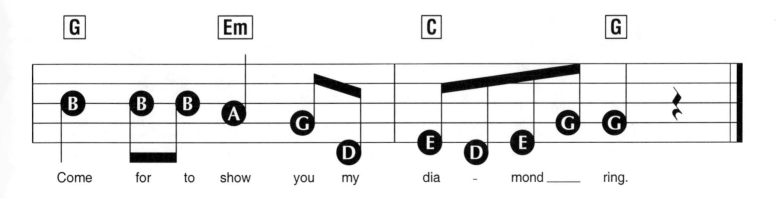

Bury Me Not
on the Lone Prairie

Registration 4
Rhythm: Country or Fox Trot

Words based on the poem "The Ocean Burial" by Rev. Edwin H. Chapin
Music by Ossian N. Dodge

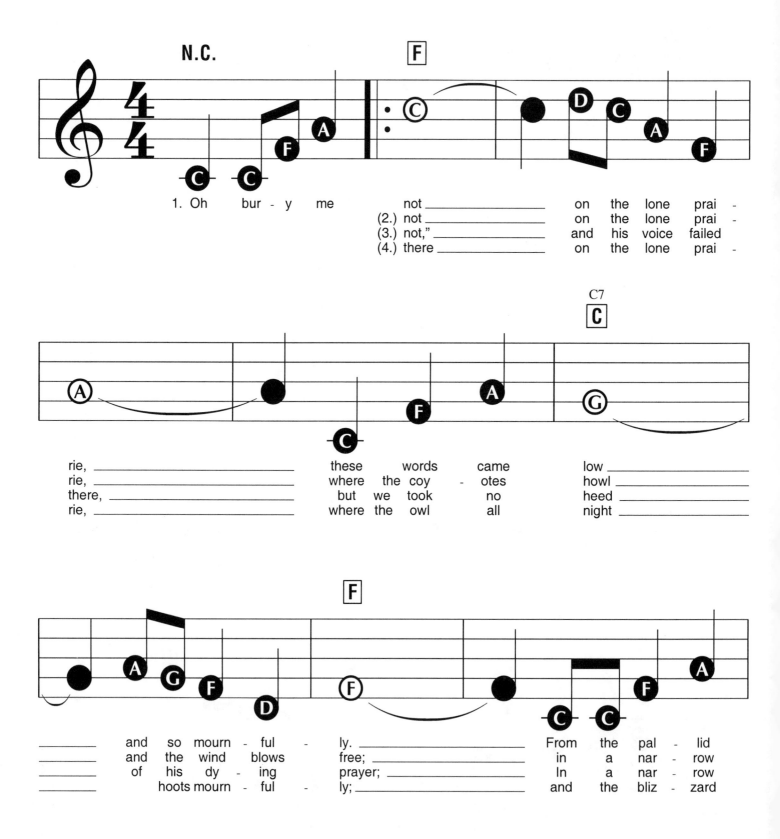

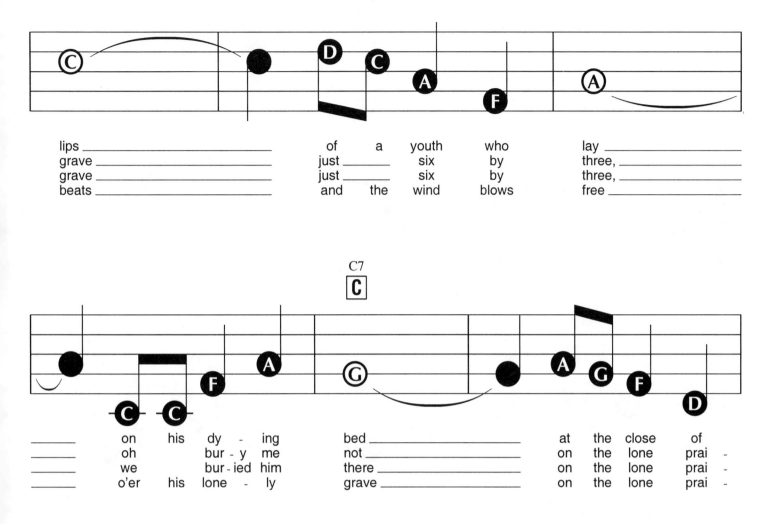

lips _____	of	a	youth	who	lay _____
grave _____	just _____	six	by	three, _____
grave _____	just _____	six	by	three, _____
beats _____	and	the	wind	blows	free _____

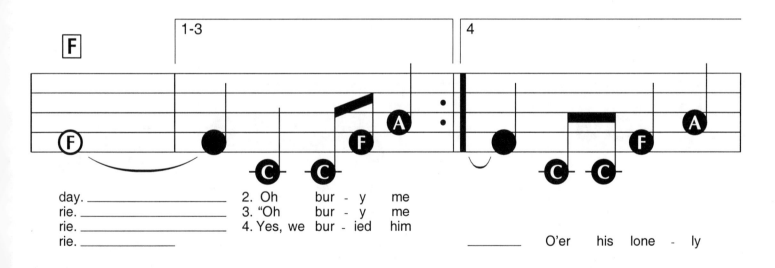

_____	on	his	dy -	ing	bed _____	at	the	close	of
_____	oh	bur - y	me	not _____	on	the	lone	prai -
_____	we	bur-ied him	there _____	on	the	lone	prai -
_____	o'er	his	lone -	ly	grave _____	on	the	lone	prai -

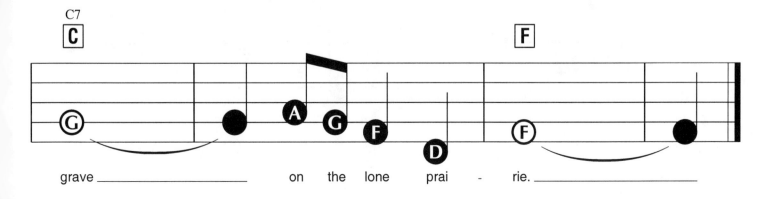

day. _____	2. Oh	bur - y	me
rie. _____	3. "Oh	bur - y	me
rie. _____	4. Yes, we	bur - ied	him
rie. _____			

_____ O'er his lone - ly

grave _____ on the lone prai - rie. _____

Cindy

Registration 3
Rhythm: Fox Trot or Swing

Southern Appalachian Folksong

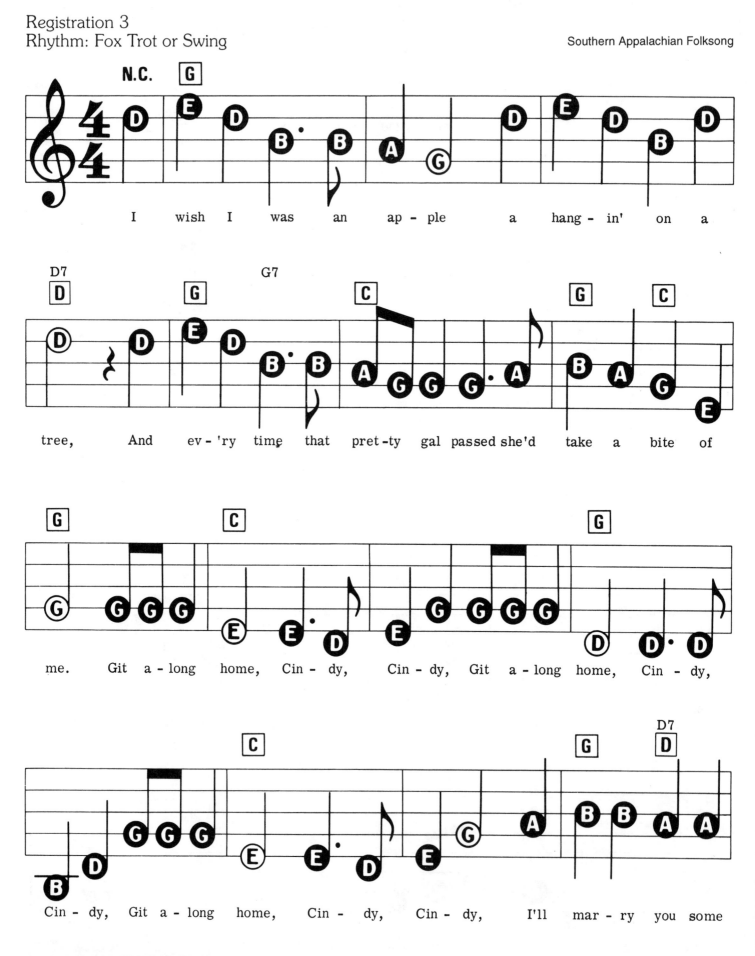

23

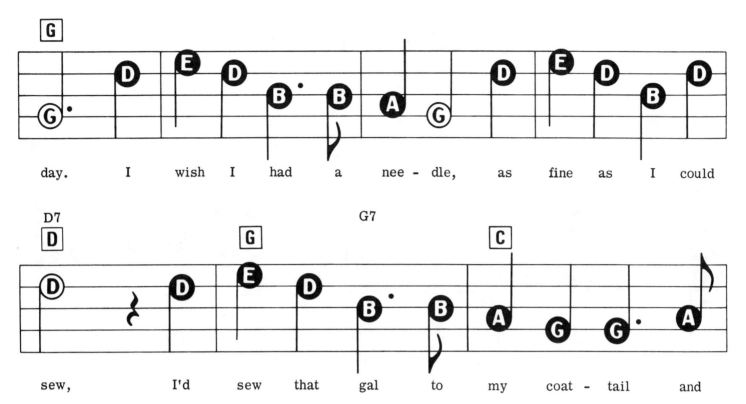

day. I wish I had a nee - dle, as fine as I could

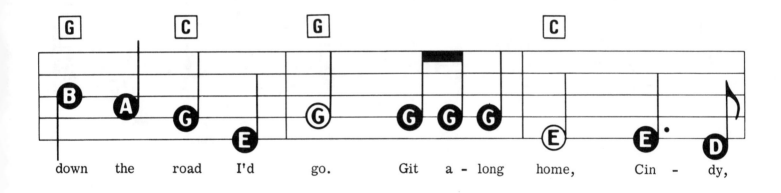

sew, I'd sew that gal to my coat - tail and

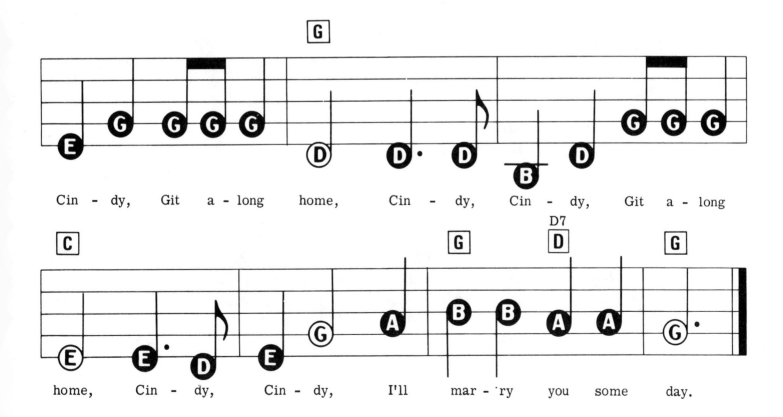

down the road I'd go. Git a - long home, Cin - dy,

Cin - dy, Git a - long home, Cin - dy, Cin - dy, Git a - long

home, Cin - dy, Cin - dy, I'll mar - ry you some day.

(Oh, My Darling)
Clementine

Registration 5
Rhythm: Waltz

Words and Music by
Percy Montrose

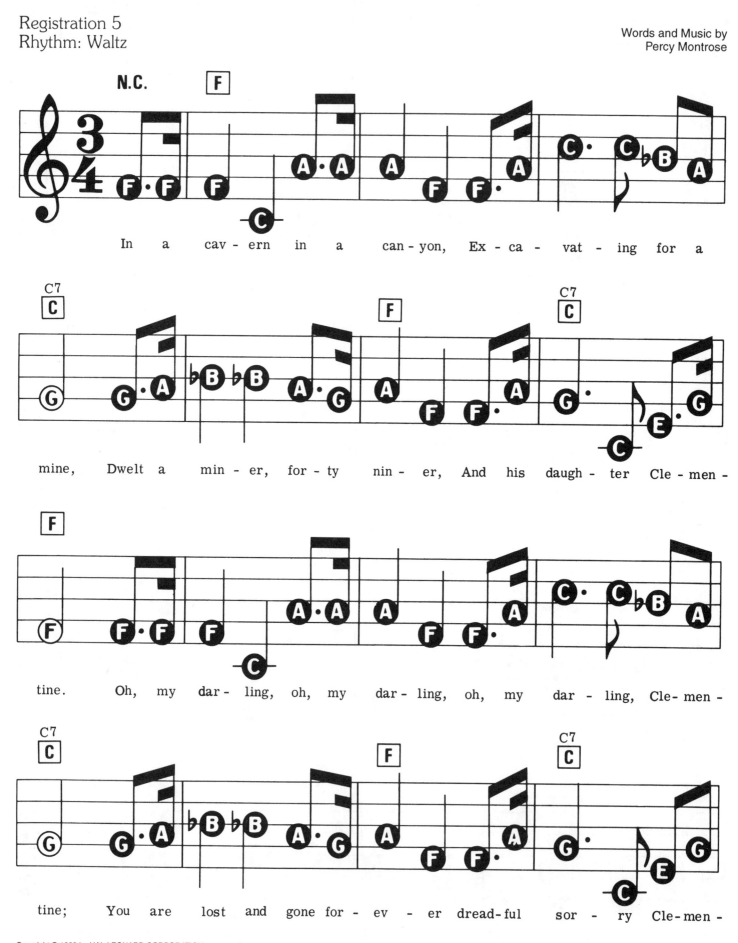

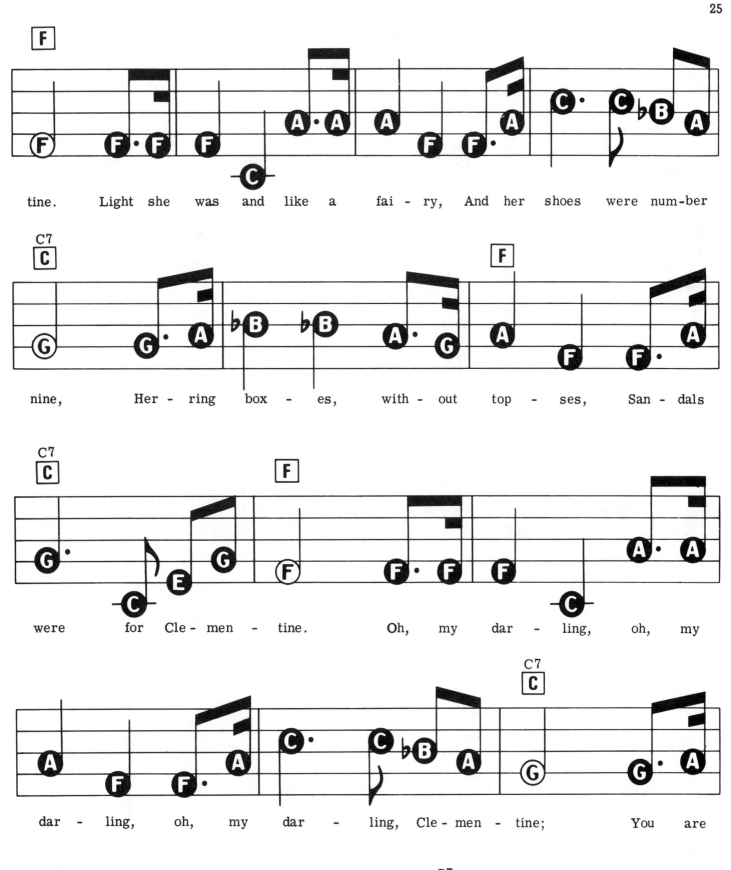

tine. Light she was and like a fai – ry, And her shoes were num-ber

nine, Her – ring box – es, with – out top – ses, San – dals

were for Cle – men – tine. Oh, my dar – ling, oh, my

dar – ling, oh, my dar – ling, Cle – men – tine; You are

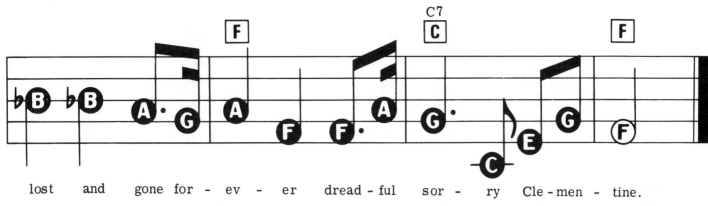

lost and gone for – ev – er dread-ful sor – ry Cle – men – tine.

The Cruel War Is Raging

Registration 8
Rhythm: Fox Trot

American Folksong

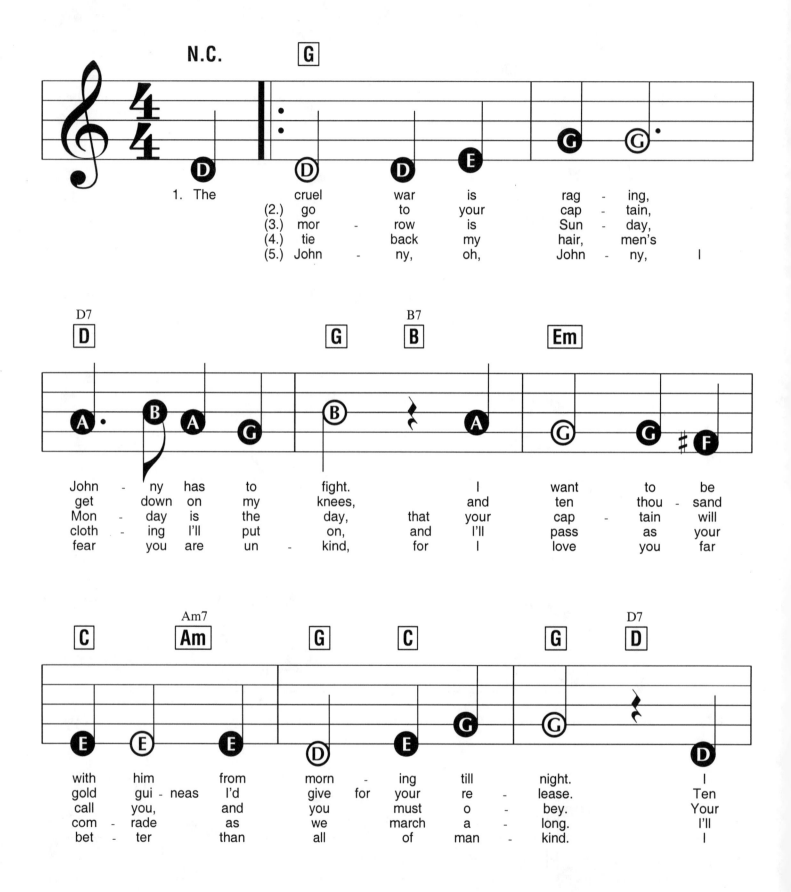

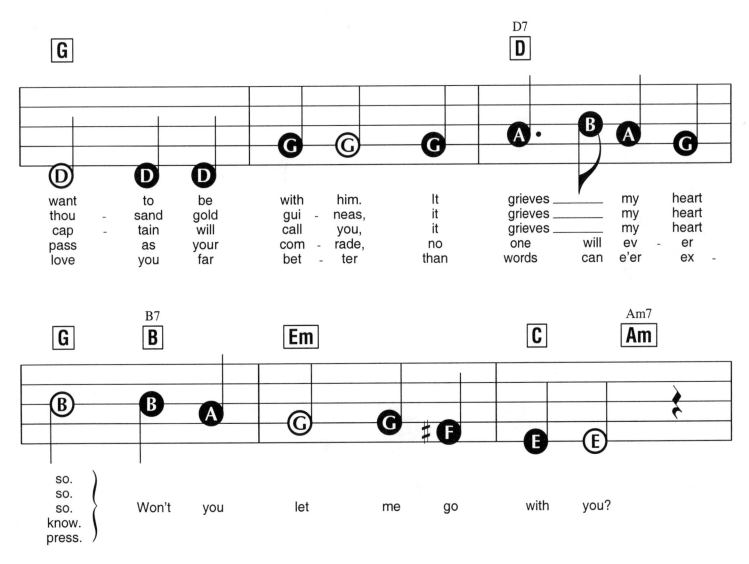

want to be with him. It grieves _____ my heart
thou - sand be gold gui - neas, it grieves _____ my heart
cap - tain will call you, it grieves _____ my heart
pass - as your com - rade, no one will ev - er
love you far bet - ter than words can e'er ex -

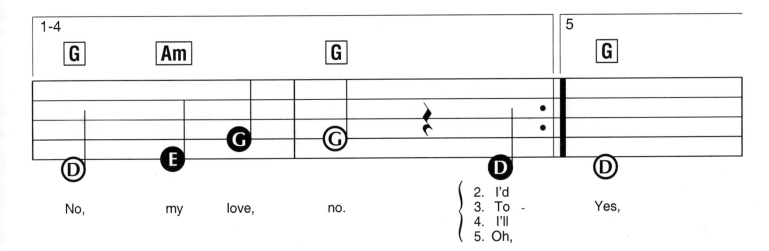

so.
so.
so.   Won't you   let   me   go   with   you?
know.
press.

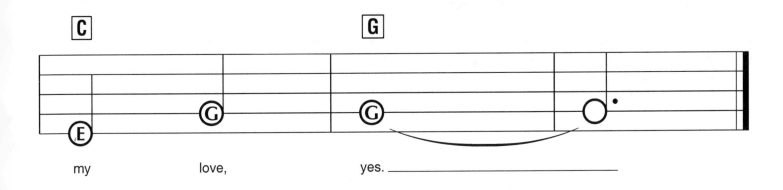

No,   my   love,   no.

2. I'd
3. To -   Yes,
4. I'll
5. Oh,

my   love,   yes. _____

Deep River

Registration 8
Rhythm: Ballad or Fox Trot

African-American Spiritual
Based on Joshua 3

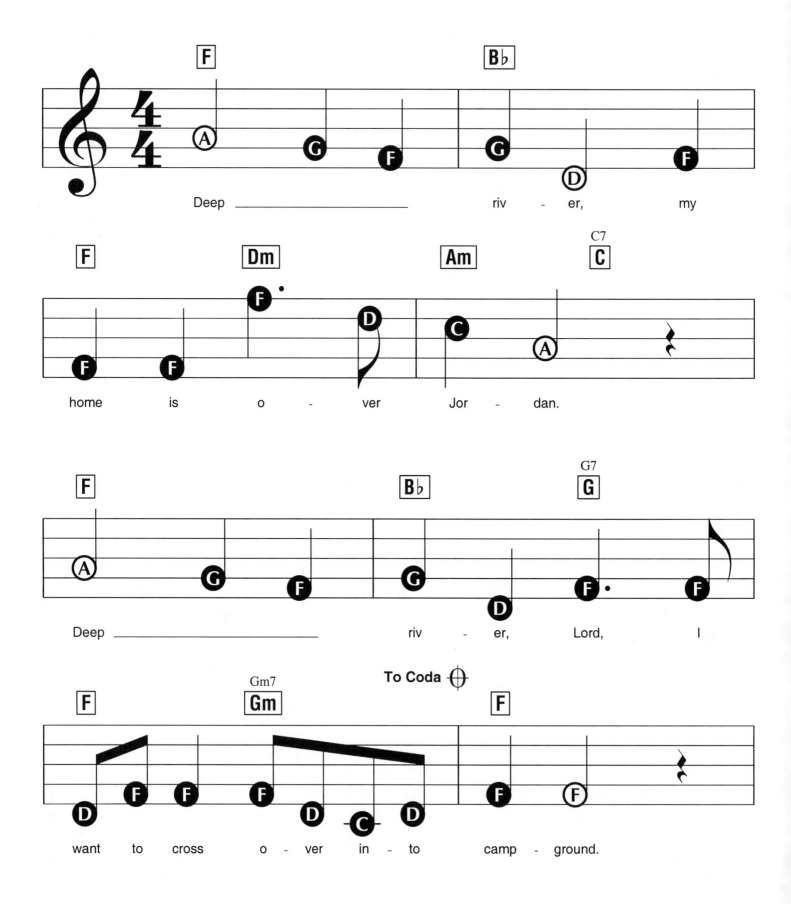

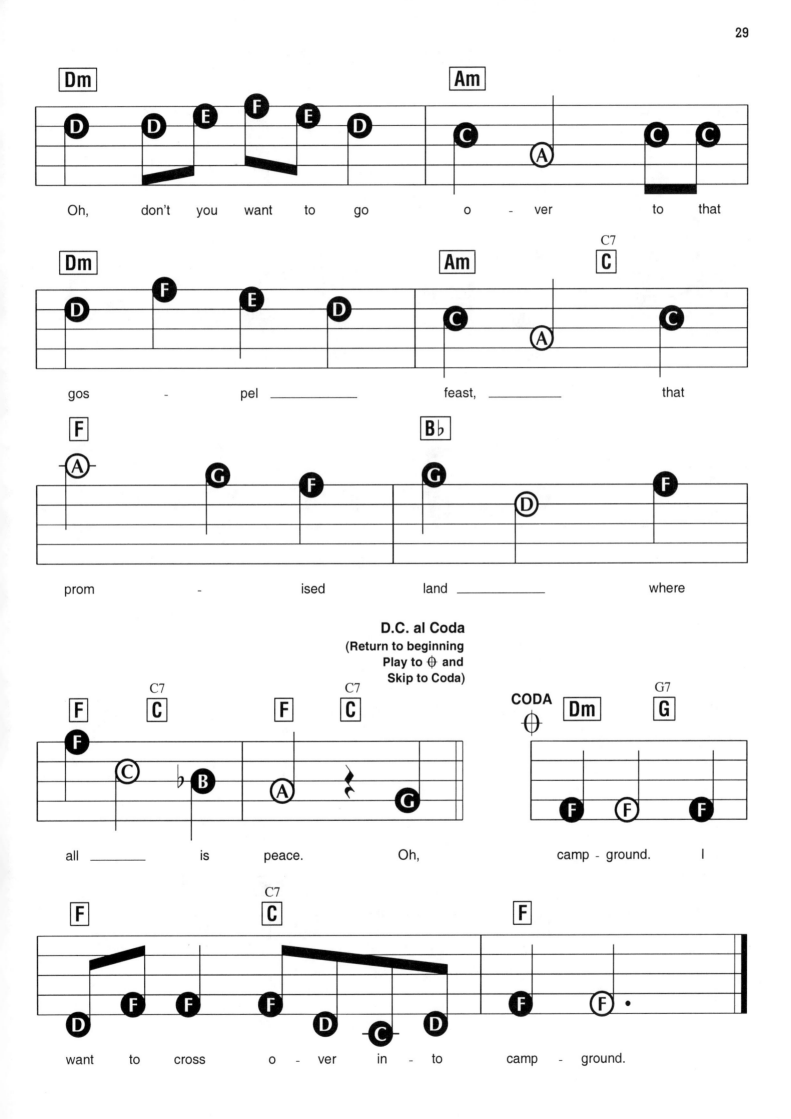

Didn't My Lord Deliver Daniel?

Registration 2
Rhythm: Rock or 8 Beat

Story from the Book Of Daniel, Chapter 6
African-American Spiritual

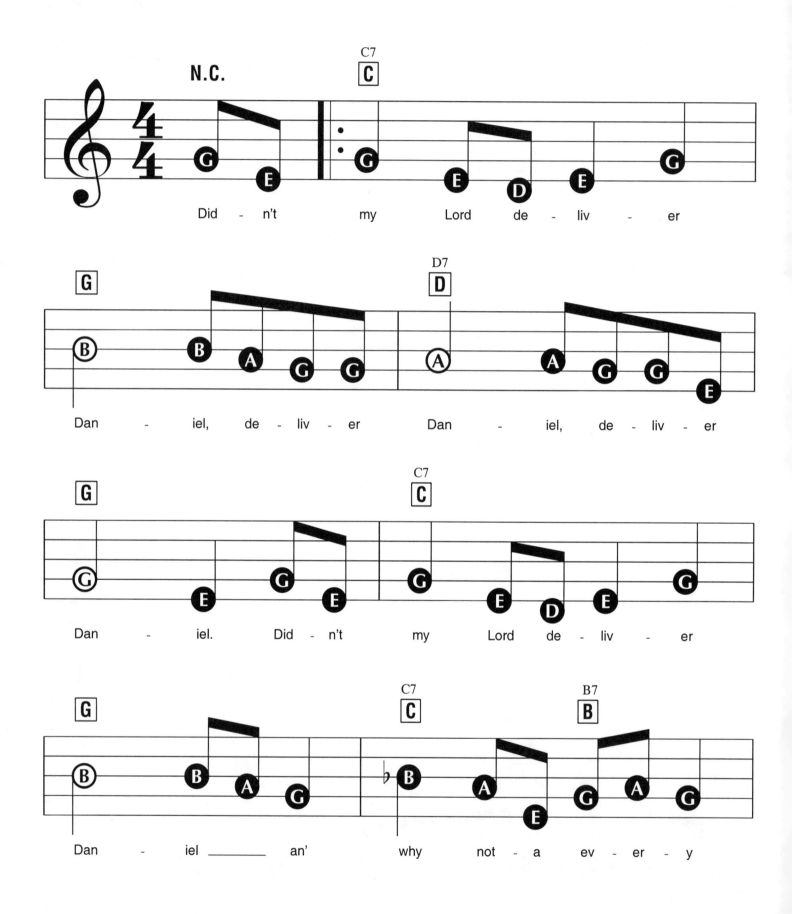

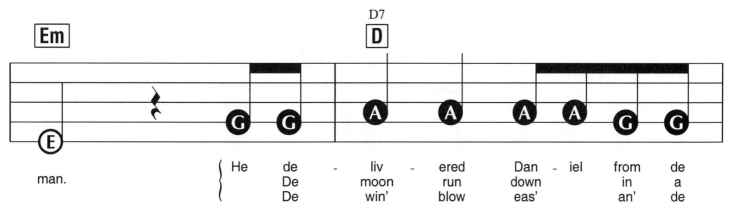

man.

He de - liv - ered Dan - iel from de
De moon run down from in a
De win' blow eas' an' de

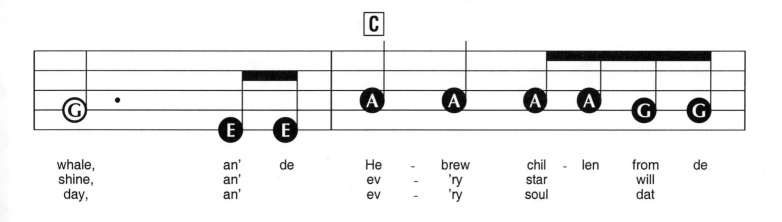

li - on's den, Jon - ah from de bel - ly of de
pur - ple stream de sun for bear to
win' blow wes', it blow like de judg - a - ment _____

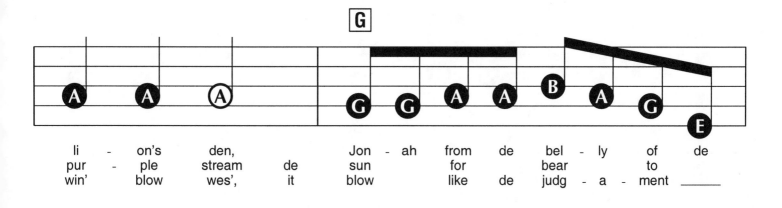

whale, an' de He - brew chil - len from de
shine, an' ev - 'ry star will
day, an' ev - 'ry soul dat

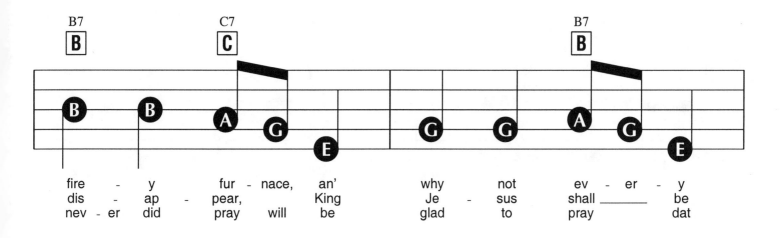

fire - y fur - nace, an' why not ev - er - y
dis - ap - pear, King Je - sus shall _____ be
nev - er did pray will be glad to pray dat

32

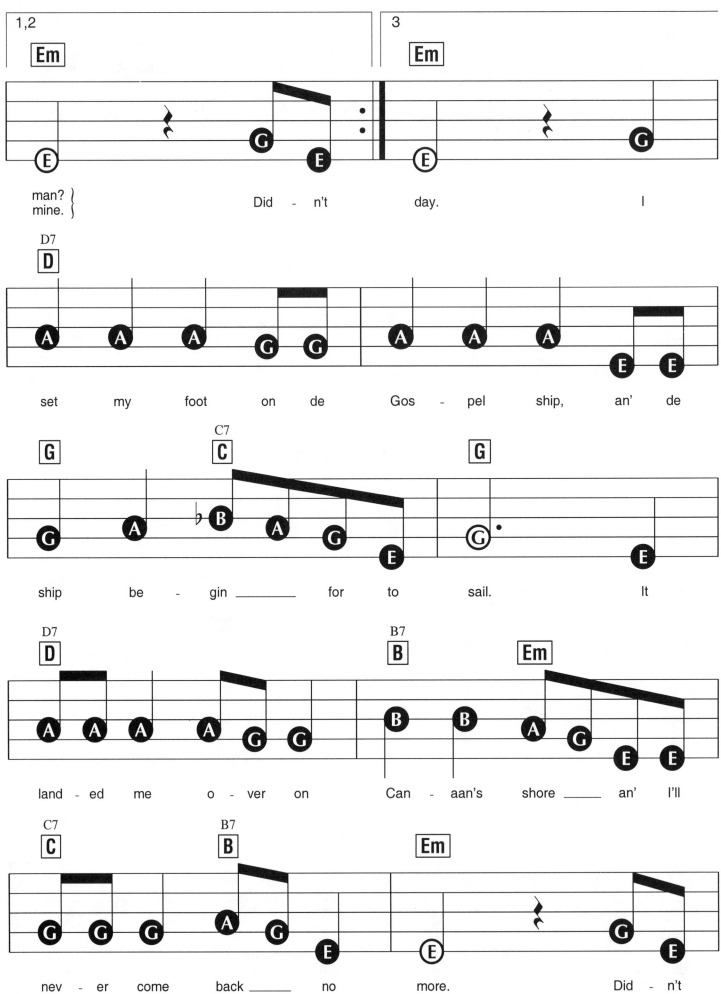

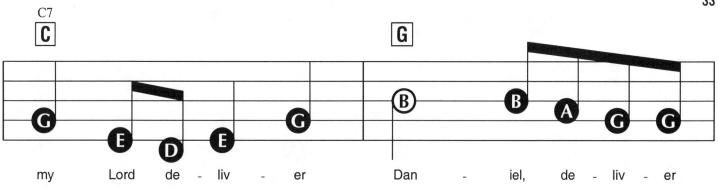

my Lord de - liv - er Dan - iel, de - liv - er

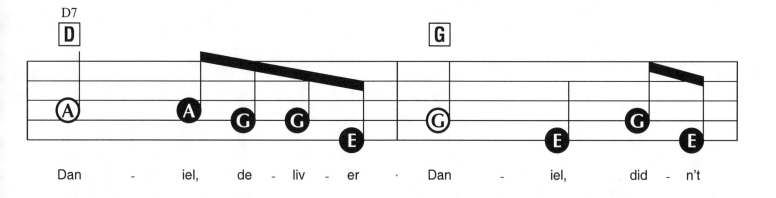

Dan - iel, de - liv - er Dan - iel, did - n't

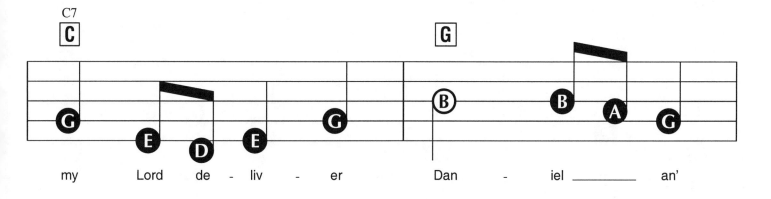

my Lord de - liv - er Dan - iel _____ an'

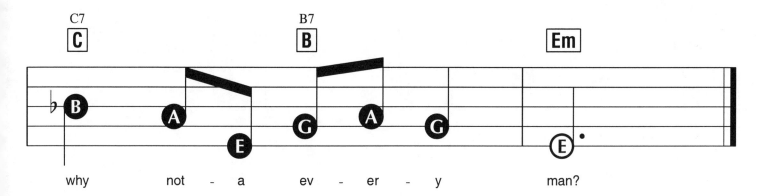

why not - a ev - er - y man?

Down in the Valley

Registration 10
Rhythm: Waltz

Traditional American Folksong

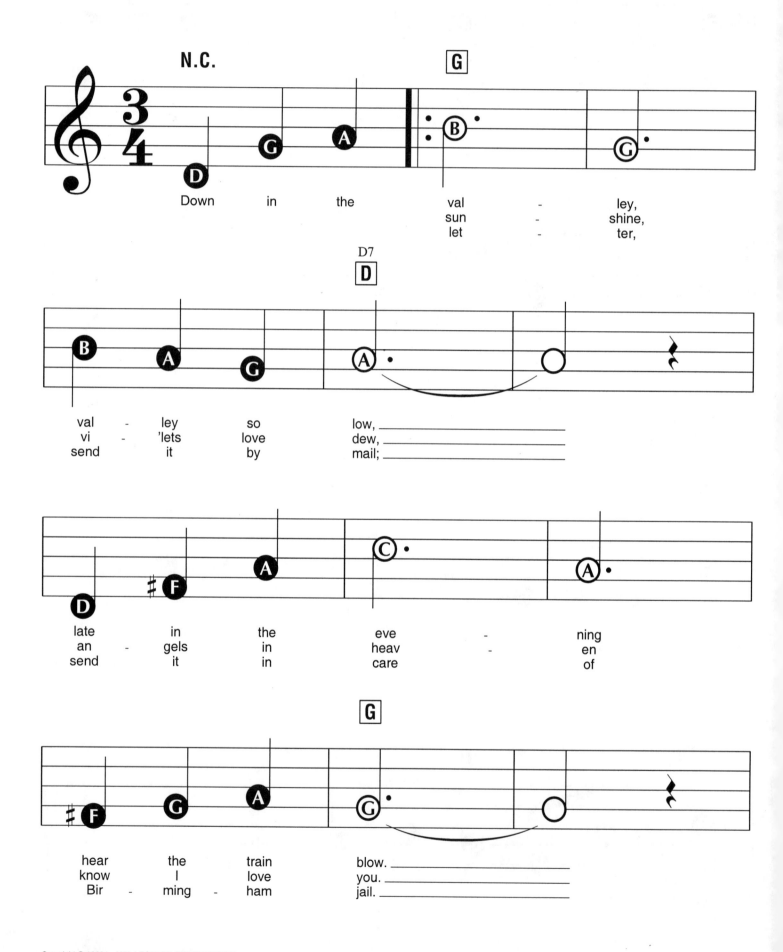

Down in the val - ley,
sun - shine,
let - ter,

val - ley so low,
vi - 'lets love dew,
send it by mail;

late in the eve - ning
an - gels in heav - en
send it in care of

hear the train blow.
know I love you.
Bir - ming - ham jail.

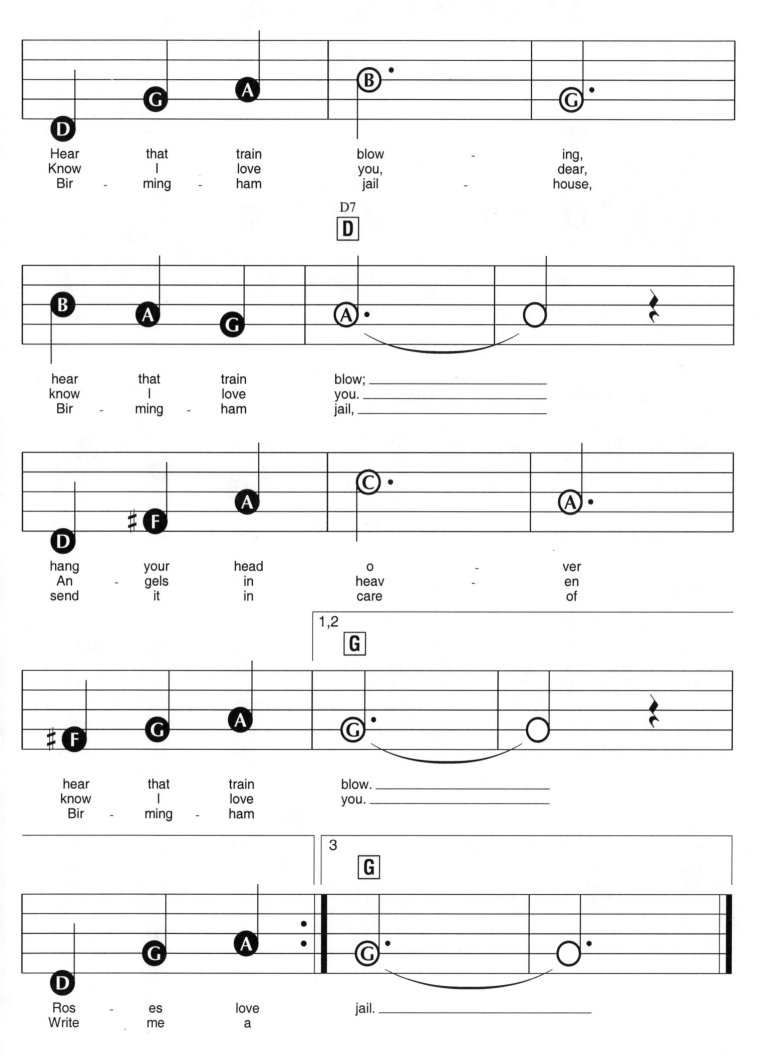

The Drunken Sailor

Registration 4
Rhythm: Fox Trot

American Sea Chantey

Dm

1. What shall we do with the drunk - en sail - or?
2. Put him in the long boat till he's so - ber,

3.-5. *(See additional lyrics)*

C

What shall we do with the drunk - en sail - or?
Put him in the long boat till he's so - ber,

Dm

What shall we do with the drunk - en sail - or?
Put him in the long boat till he's so - ber,

C   **Dm**

Ear - lye in the morn - ing.

Chorus

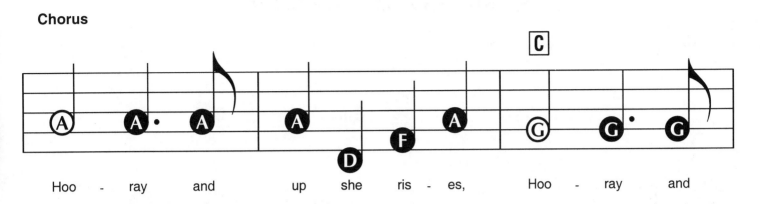

Hoo - ray and up she ris - es, Hoo - ray and

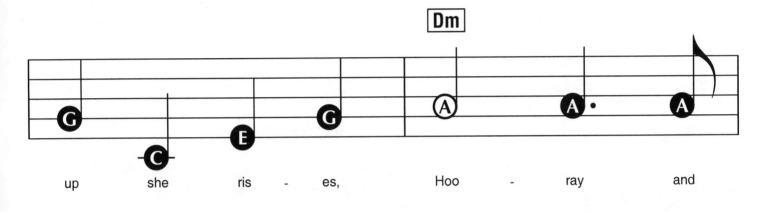

up she ris - es, Hoo - ray and

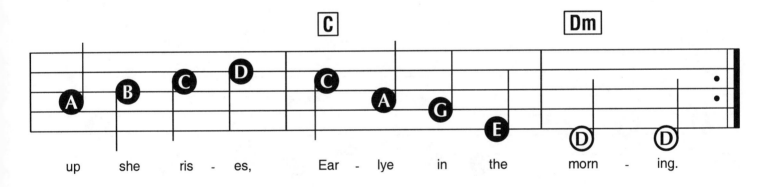

up she ris - es, Ear - lye in the morn - ing.

Additional Lyrics

3. Pull out the plug and wet him all over,
   Pull out the plug and wet him all over,
   Pull out the plug and wet him all over,
   Earlye in the morning.
   Chorus

4. Tie him to the top mast when she's under,
   Tie him to the top mast when she's under,
   Tie him to the top mast when she's under,
   Earlye in the morning.
   Chorus

5. Put him in the scuppers with the hosepipe on him,
   Put him in the scuppers with the hosepipe on him,
   Put him in the scuppers with the hosepipe on him,
   Earlye in the morning.
   Chorus

The Erie Canal

Registration 2
Rhythm: Fox Trot

Traditional New York Work Song

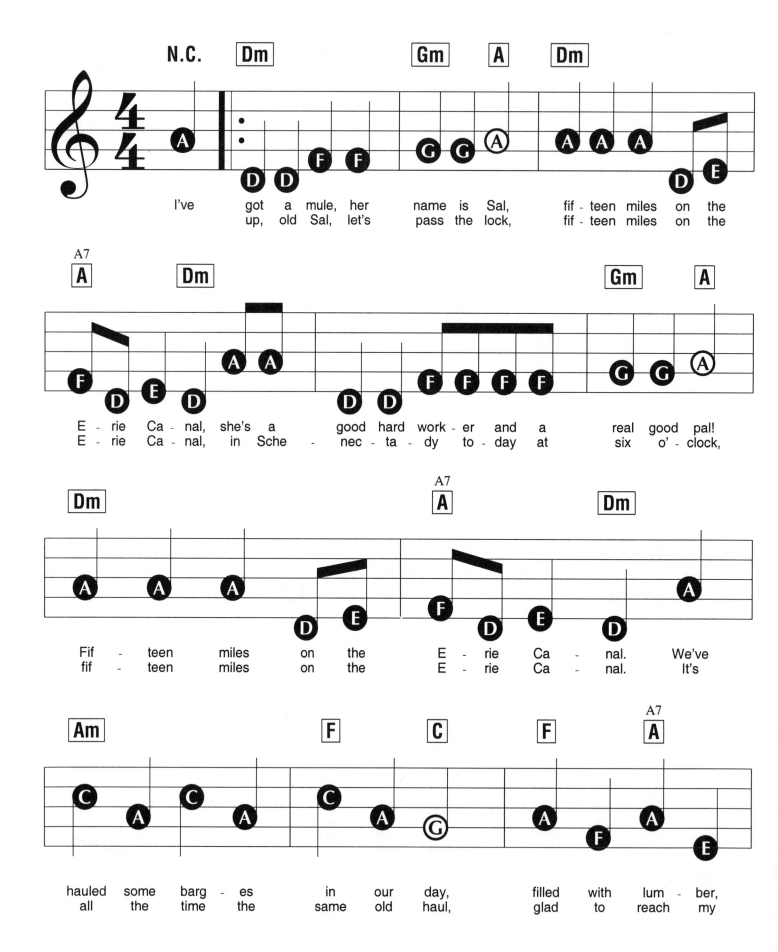

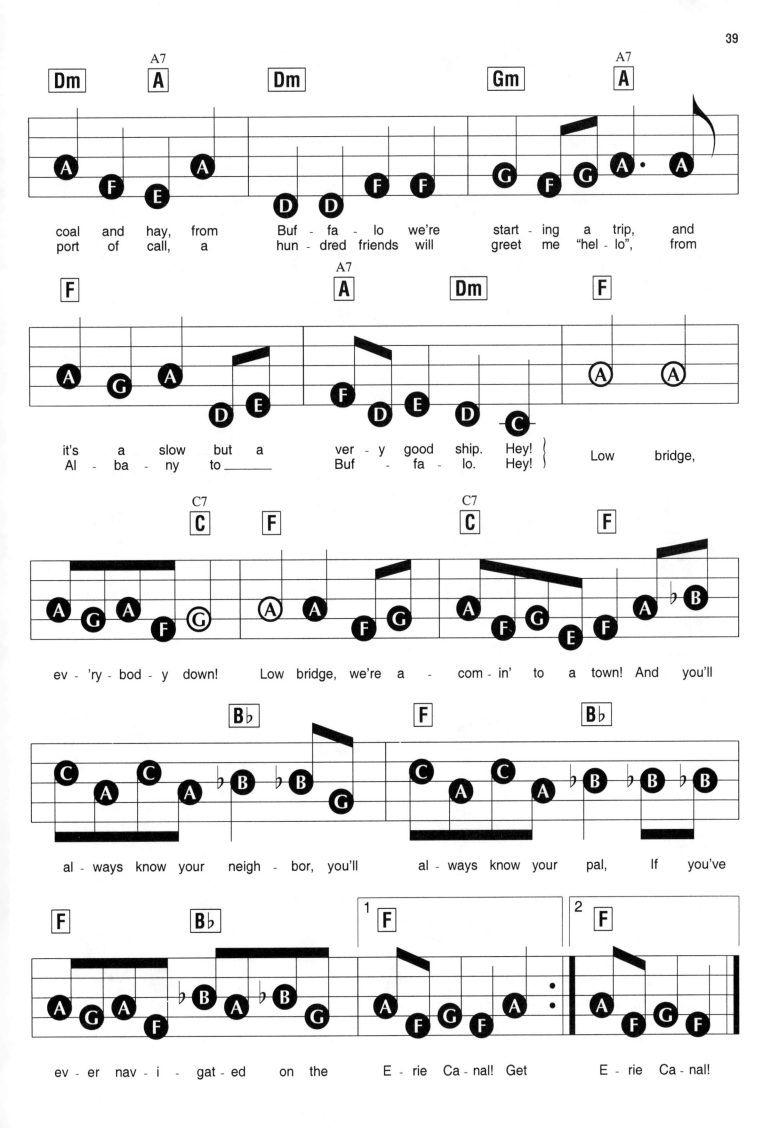

Every Time I Feel the Spirit

Registration 7
Rhythm: Rock or 8 Beat

African-American Spiritual

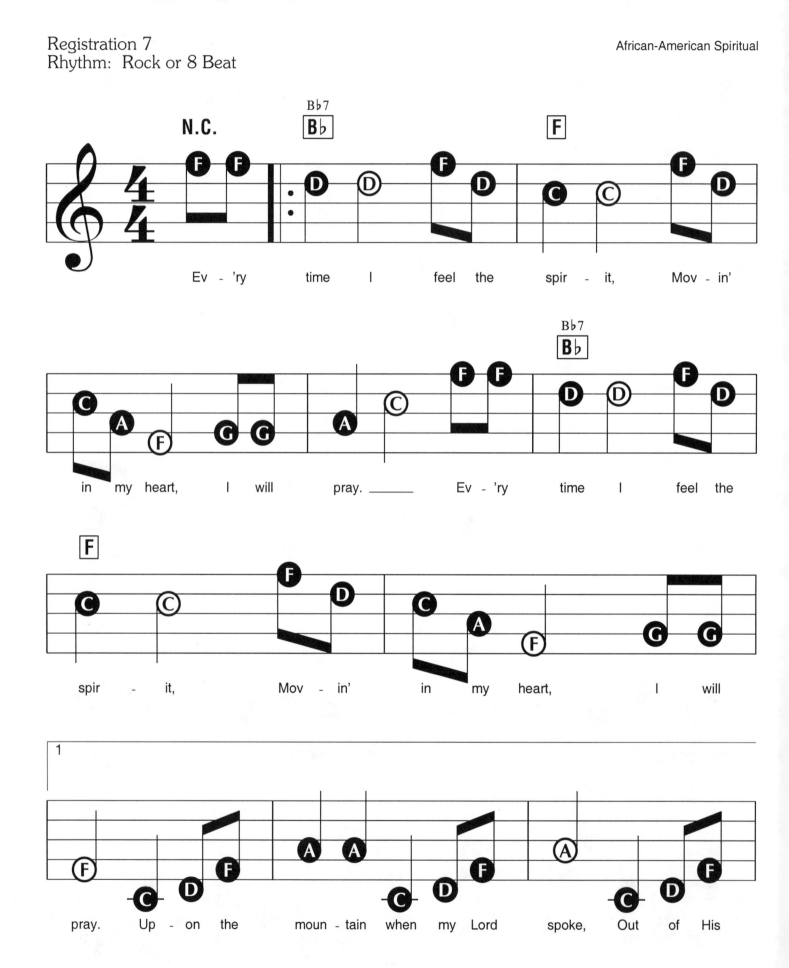

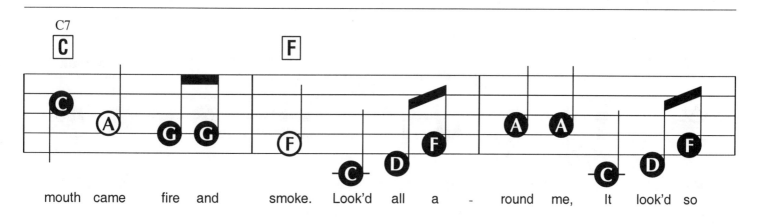

mouth came fire and smoke. Look'd all a - round me, It look'd so

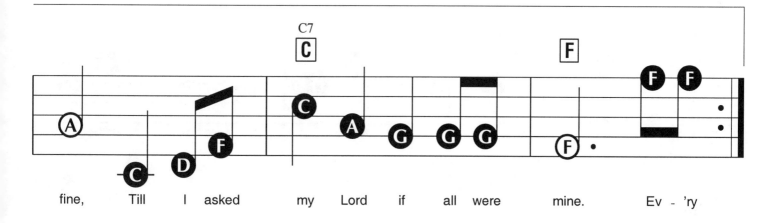

fine, Till I asked my Lord if all were mine. Ev - 'ry

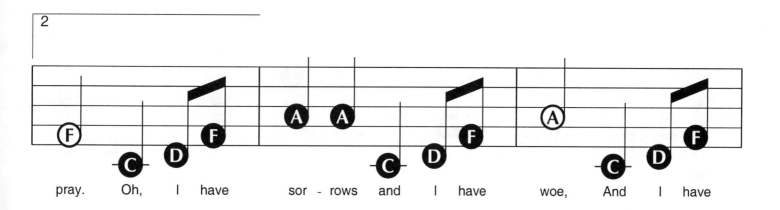

pray. Oh, I have sor - rows and I have woe, And I have

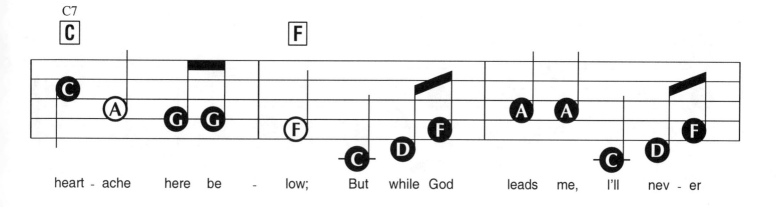

heart - ache here be - low; But while God leads me, I'll nev - er

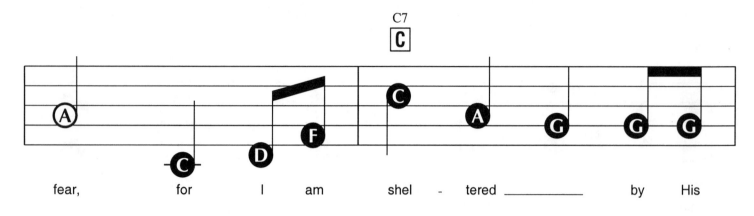

fear, for I am shel - tered _____ by His

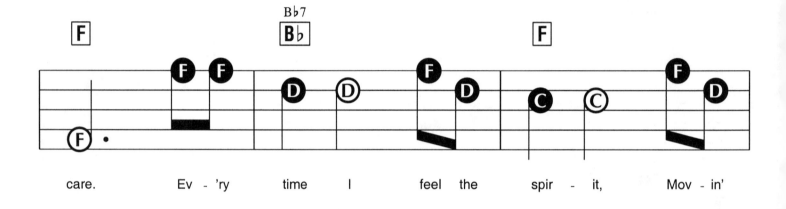

care. Ev - 'ry time I feel the spir - it, Mov - in'

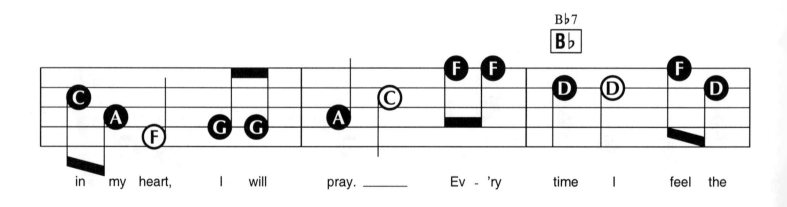

in my heart, I will pray. _____ Ev - 'ry time I feel the

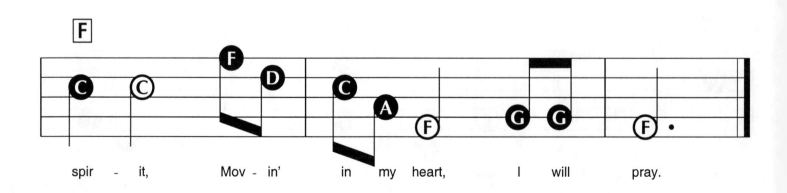

spir - it, Mov - in' in my heart, I will pray.

Hush, Little Baby

Registration 1
Rhythm: 8 Beat or Pops

Carolina Folk Lullaby

Hush, lit - tle ba - by, don't say a word;
If that dia - mond ring turns brass,
If that bil - ly goat won't pull,
If that dog named Rover won't bark

Pa - pa's gon - na buy you a mock - ing - bird. And
Pa - pa's gon - na buy you a look - ing glass. And
Pa - pa's gon - na buy you a cart and bull. And
Pa - pa's gon - na buy you a horse and cart. And

if that mock - ing - bird won't sing,
if that look - ing glass gets broke,
if that cart and bull turn over,
if that horse and cart fall down,

Pa - pa's gon - na buy you a dia - mond ring.
Pa - pa's gon - na buy you a bil - ly goat.
Pa - pa's gon - na buy you a dog named Rover.
you'll be the sweetest lit - tle baby in town.

Frankie and Johnny

Registration 4
Rhythm: Swing

Anonymous Blues Ballad

1. Frank - ie and John - ny were   lov - ers.   Oh, Lord - y how they could
2. - 13. (*See additional lyrics*)

love.   Swore to be   true to each   oth - er,   just as

true   as   stars a - bove. He was her   man, _____

_____   but he done   her   wrong. _____

Additional Lyrics

2. Frankie she was a good woman
   As everybody know,
   Spent a hundred dollars
   Just to buy her man some clothes.
   He was her man, but he was doing her wrong.

3. Frankie went down to the corner
   Just for a bucket of beer,
   Said: "Mr. bartender
   Has my loving Johnny been here?
   "He was my man, but he's a-doing me wrong."

4. "Now I don't want to tell you no stories
   And I don't want to tell you no lies
   I saw your man about an hour ago
   With a gal named Nellie Bligh
   He was your man, but he's a-doing you wrong."

5. Frankie she went down to the hotel
   Didn't go there for fun,
   Underneath her kimono
   She carried a forty-four gun.
   He was her man, but he was doing her wrong.

6. Frankie looked over the transom
   To see what she could spy,
   There sat Johnny on the sofa
   Just loving up Nellie Bligh.
   He was her man, but he was doing her wrong.

7. Frankie got down from that high stool
   She didn't want to see no more;
   Rooty-toot-toot three times she shot
   Right through that hardwood door.
   He was her man, but he was doing her wrong.

8. Now the first time that Frankie shot Johnny
   He let out an awful yell,
   Second time she shot him
   There was a new man's face in hell.
   He was her man, but he was doing her wrong.

9. "Oh roll me over easy
   Roll me over slow
   Roll me over on the right side
   For the left side hurts me so."
   He was her man, but he was doing her wrong.

10. Sixteen rubber-tired carriages
    Sixteen rubber-tired hacks
    They take poor Johnny to the graveyard
    They ain't gonna bring him back.
    He was her man, but he was doing her wrong.

11. Frankie looked out of the jailhouse
    To see what she could see,
    All she could hear was a two-string bow
    Crying nearer my God to thee.
    He was her man, but he was doing her wrong.

12. Frankie she said to the sheriff
    "What do you reckon they'll do?"
    Sheriff he said "Frankie,
    "It's the electric chair for you."
    He was her man, but he was doing her wrong.

13. This story has no moral
    This story has no end
    This story only goes to show
    That there ain't no good in men!
    He was her man, but he was doing her wrong.

Git Along, Little Dogies

Registration 3
Rhythm: Waltz

Western American Cowboy Song

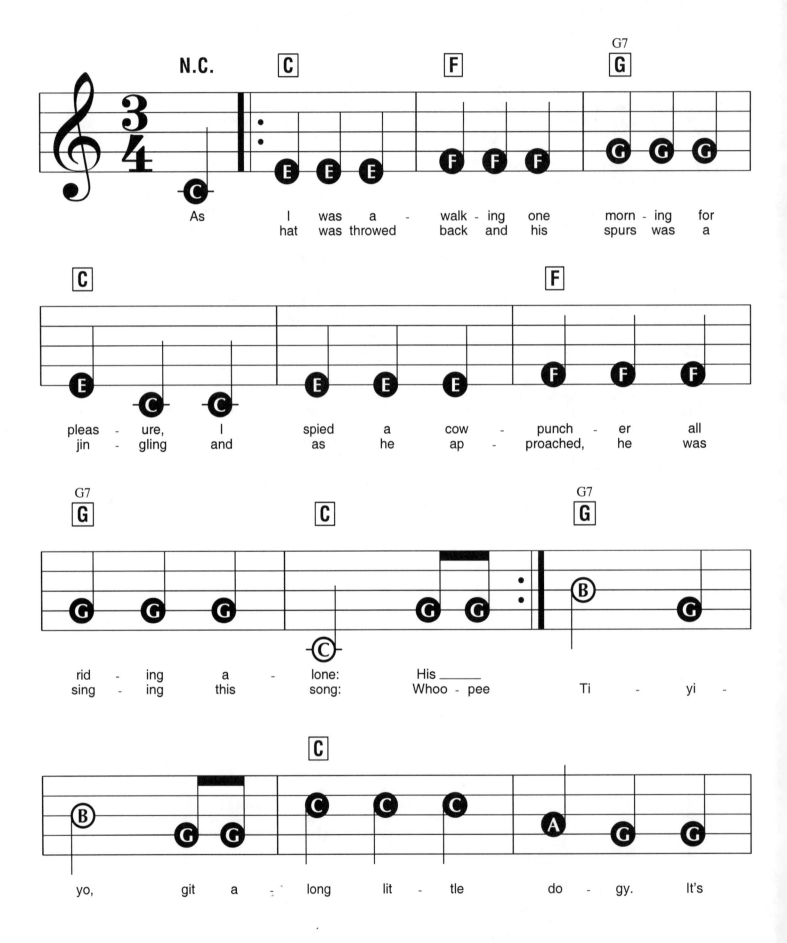

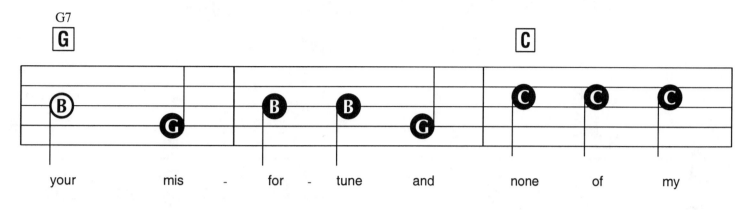

your mis - for - tune and none of my

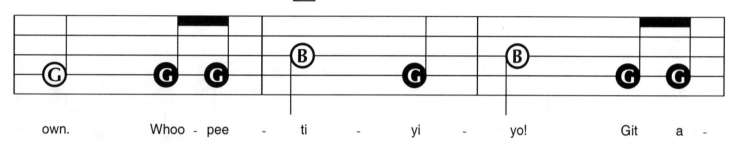

own. Whoo - pee - ti - yi - yo! Git a -

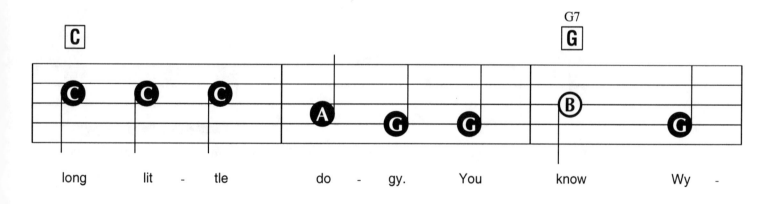

long lit - tle do - gy. You know Wy -

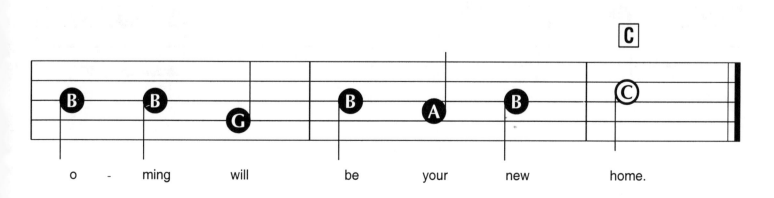

o - ming will be your new home.

He's Got the Whole World in His Hands

Registration 6
Rhythm: Swing or Rock

Traditional Spiritual

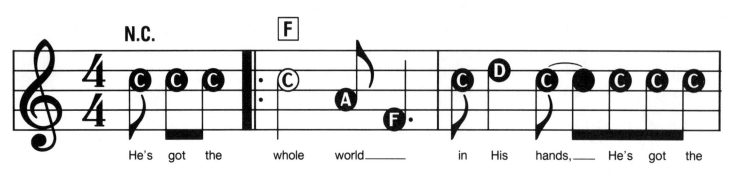

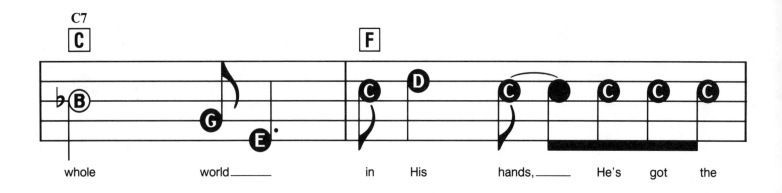

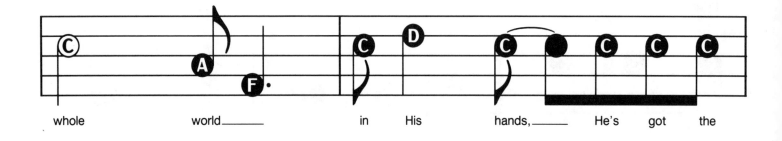

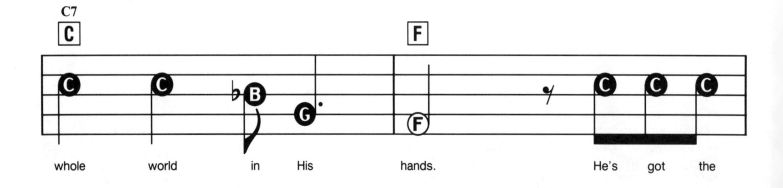

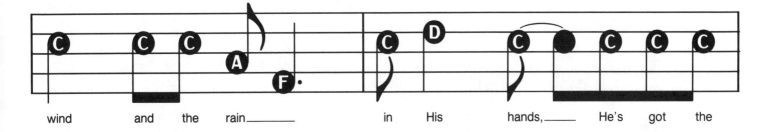

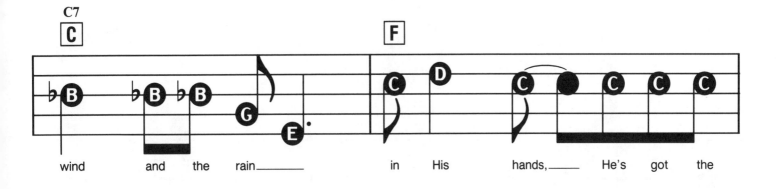

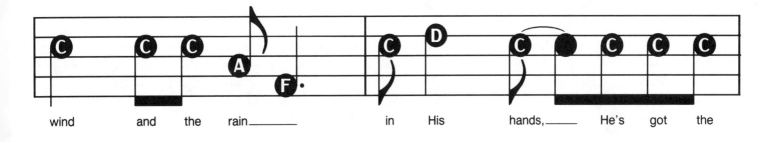

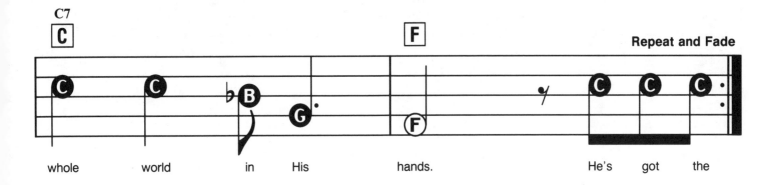

High Barbaree

Registration 9
Rhythm: Waltz

Words and Music by
Charles Dibdin

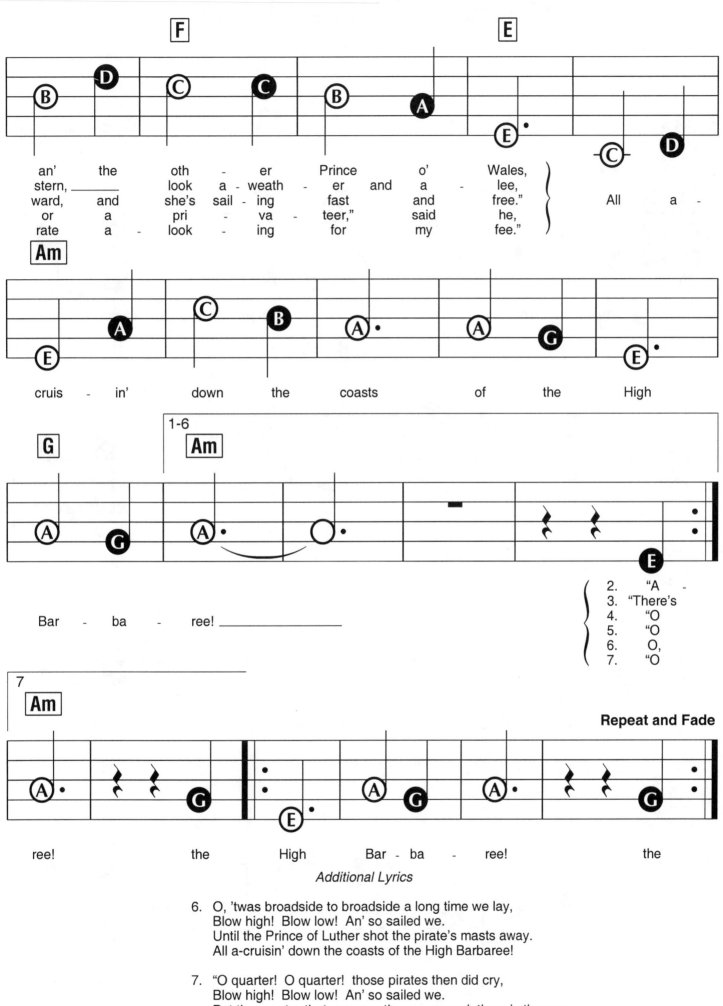

Additional Lyrics

6. O, 'twas broadside to broadside a long time we lay,
   Blow high! Blow low! An' so sailed we.
   Until the Prince of Luther shot the pirate's masts away.
   All a-cruisin' down the coasts of the High Barbaree!

7. "O quarter! O quarter! those pirates then did cry,
   Blow high! Blow low! An' so sailed we.
   But the quarter that we gave them - we sunk them in the sea.
   All a-cruisin' down the coasts of the High Barbaree!

Home on the Range

Registration 4
Rhythm: Waltz

Lyrics by Dr. Brewster Higley
Music by Dan Kelly

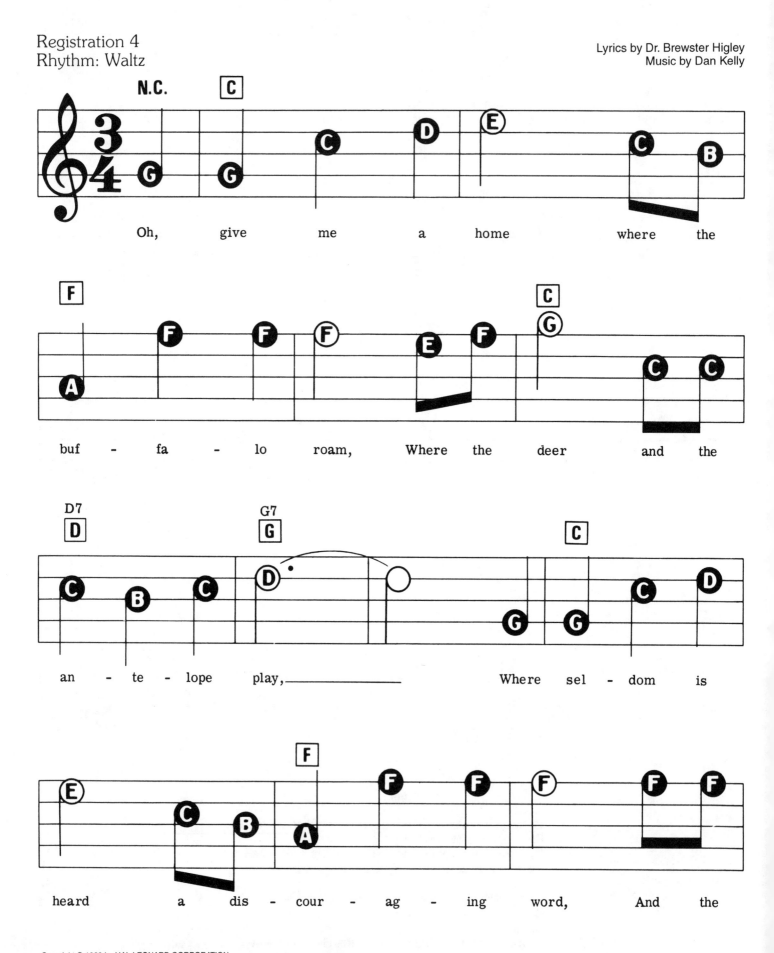

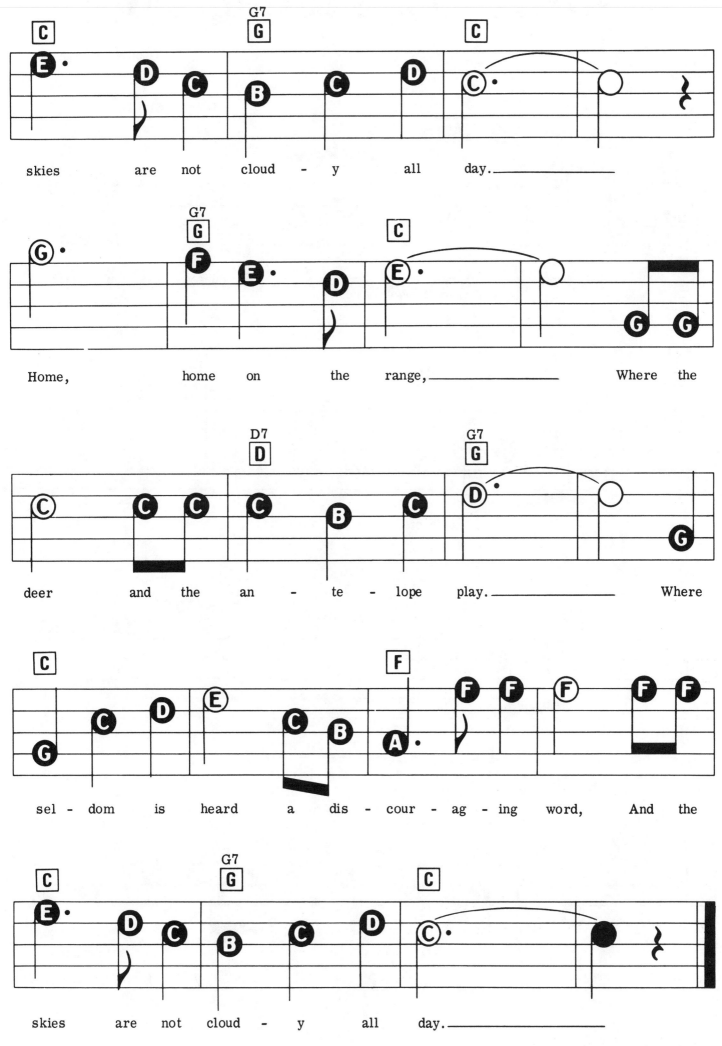

House of the Rising Sun

Registration 2
Rhythm: Waltz

Southern American Folksong

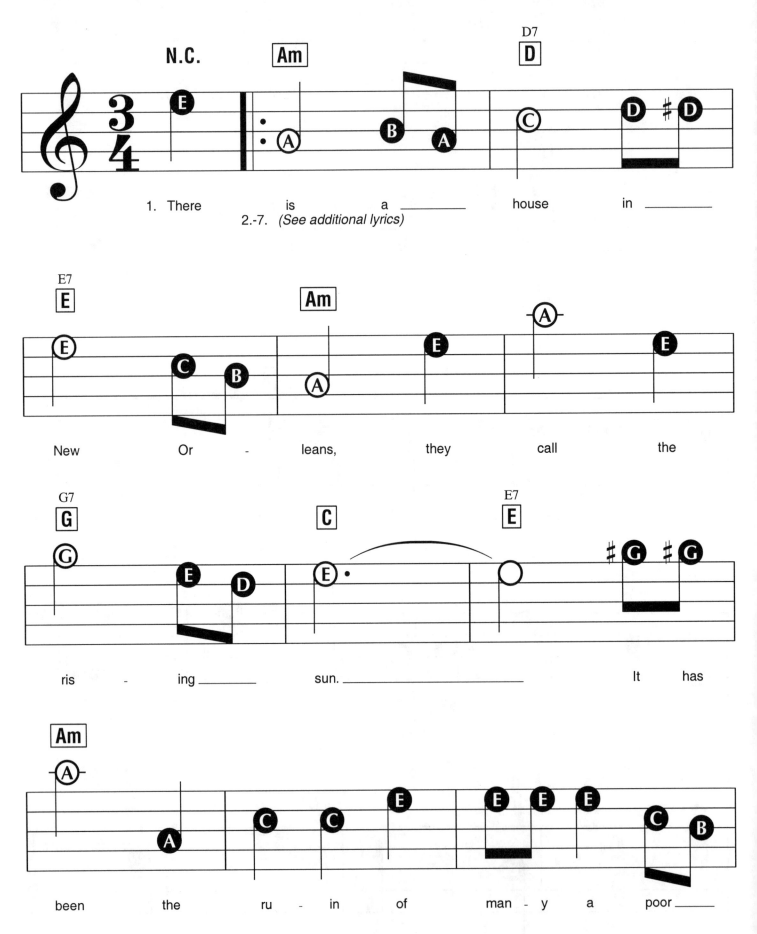

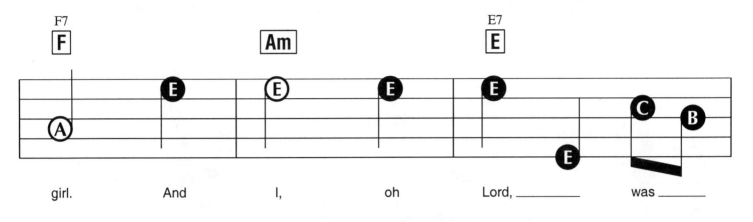

girl.   And   I,   oh   Lord, _____ was _____

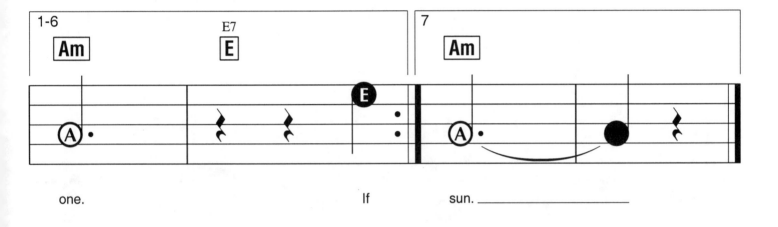

one.   If   sun. _____

Additional Lyrics

2. If I had listened to what mama said,
   I'd 'a' been at home today.
   Being so young and foolish, poor girl,
   Let a gambler lead me astray.

3. My mother, she's a tailor,
   She sells those new blue jeans.
   My sweetheart, he's a drunkard, Lord,
   Drinks down in New Orleans.

4. The only thing a drunkard needs
   Is a suitcase and a trunk.
   The only time he's satisfied
   Is when he's on a drunk.

5. Go tell my baby, sister,
   Never do like I have done.
   To shun that house in New Orleans,
   They call the Rising Sun.

6. One foot is on the platform,
   And the other one on the train.
   I'm going back to New Orleans
   To wear that ball and chain.

7. I'm going back to New Orleans,
   My race is almost run.
   Going back to end my life
   Beneath the rising sun.

How Can I Keep from Singing

Registration 2
Rhythm: Waltz

American Folk Hymn

My

life flows on in end - less song a -
through the temp - est round me rears, I
ty - rants trem - ble, sick with fear and

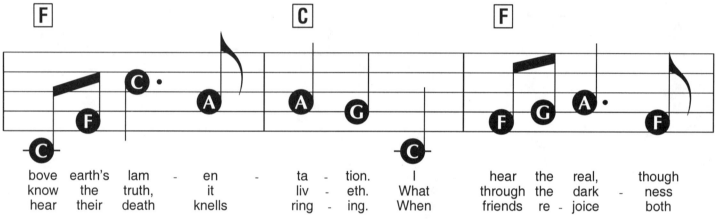

bove earth's lam - en - ta - tion. I hear the real, though
know the truth, it liv - eth. What through the dark - ness
hear their death knells ring - ing. When friends re - joice both

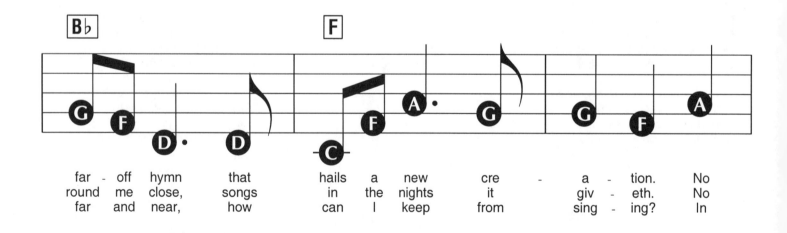

far - off hymn that hails a new cre - a - tion. No
round me close, songs that in the nights it giv - eth. No
far and near, how can I keep from sing - ing? In

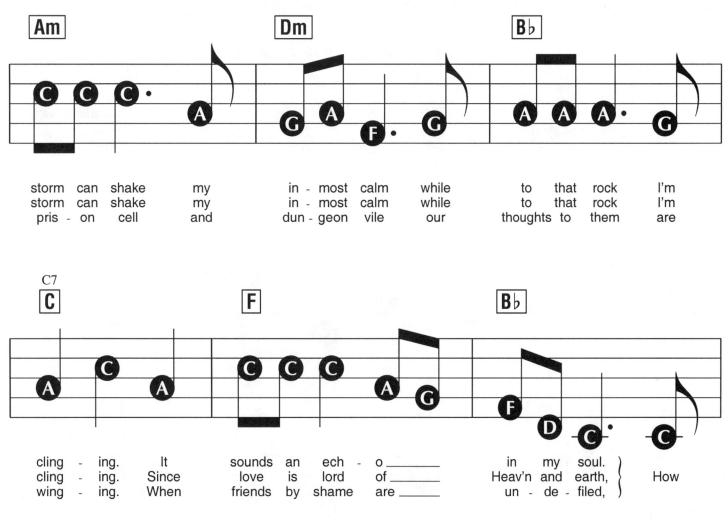

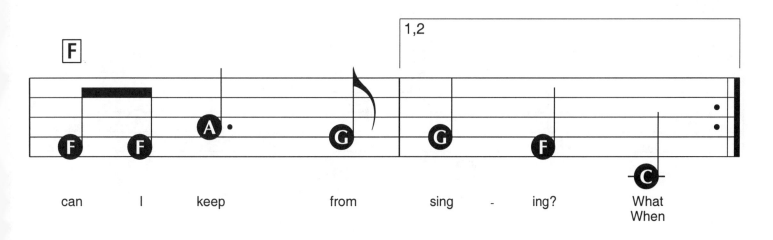

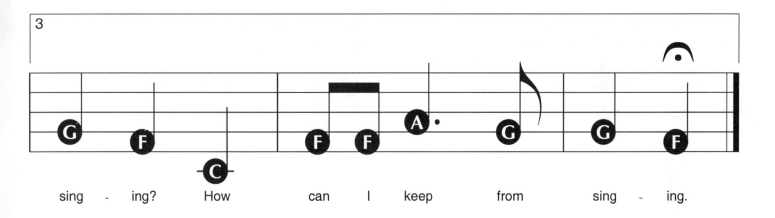

I've Been Working on the Railroad

Registration 5
Rhythm: March or Swing

American Folksong

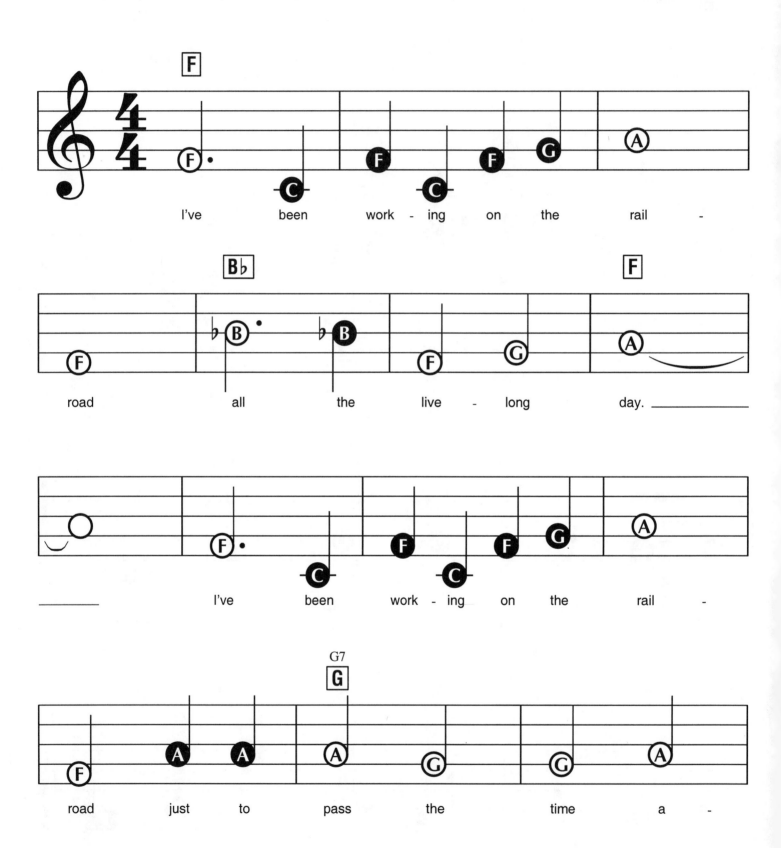

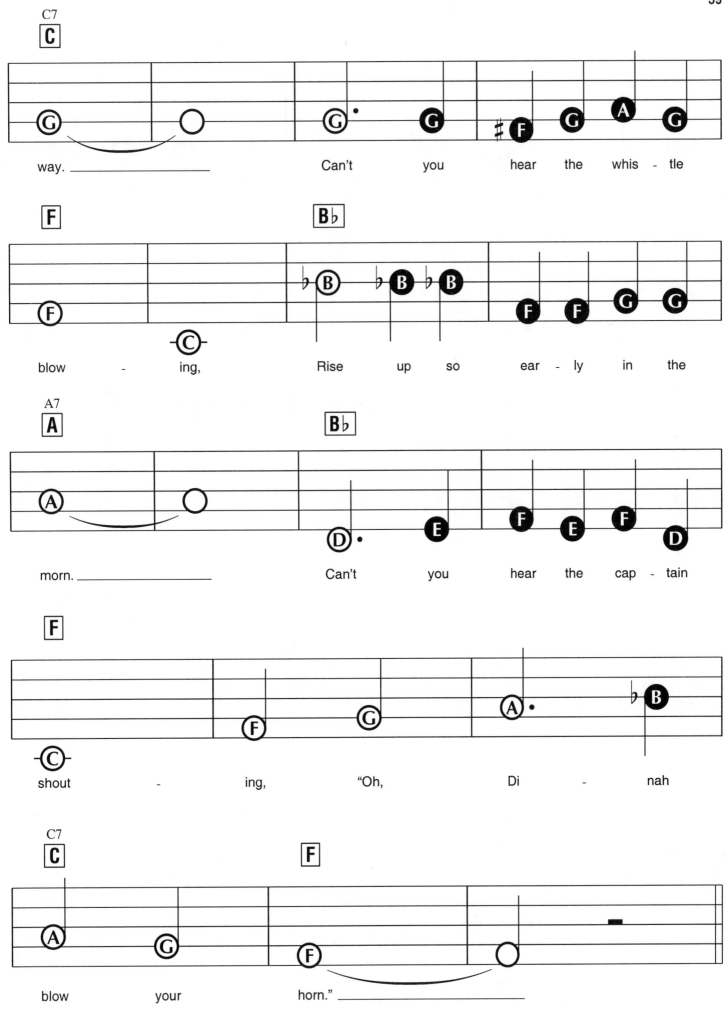

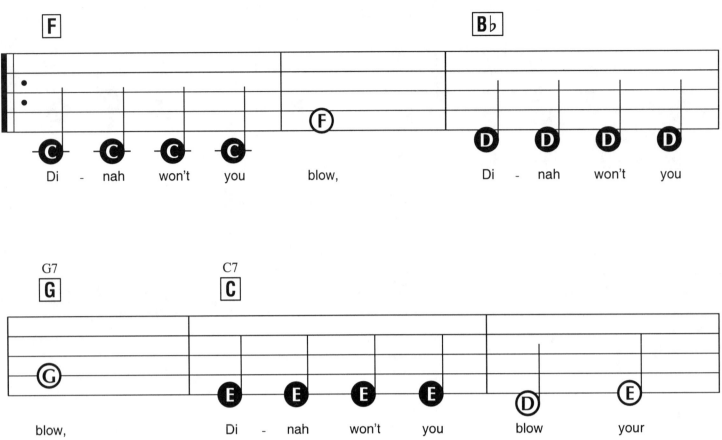

F

Bb

Di - nah won't you blow, Di - nah won't you

G7
G

C7
C

blow, Di - nah won't you blow your

1
F

horn? _____

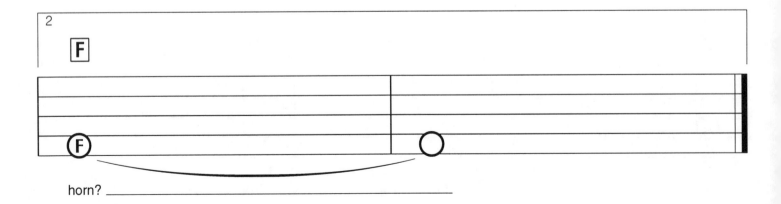

2
F

horn? _____

Li'l Liza Jane
(Go Li'l Liza)

Registration 9
Rhythm: Fox Trot or Swing

Words and Music by
Countess Ada De Lachau

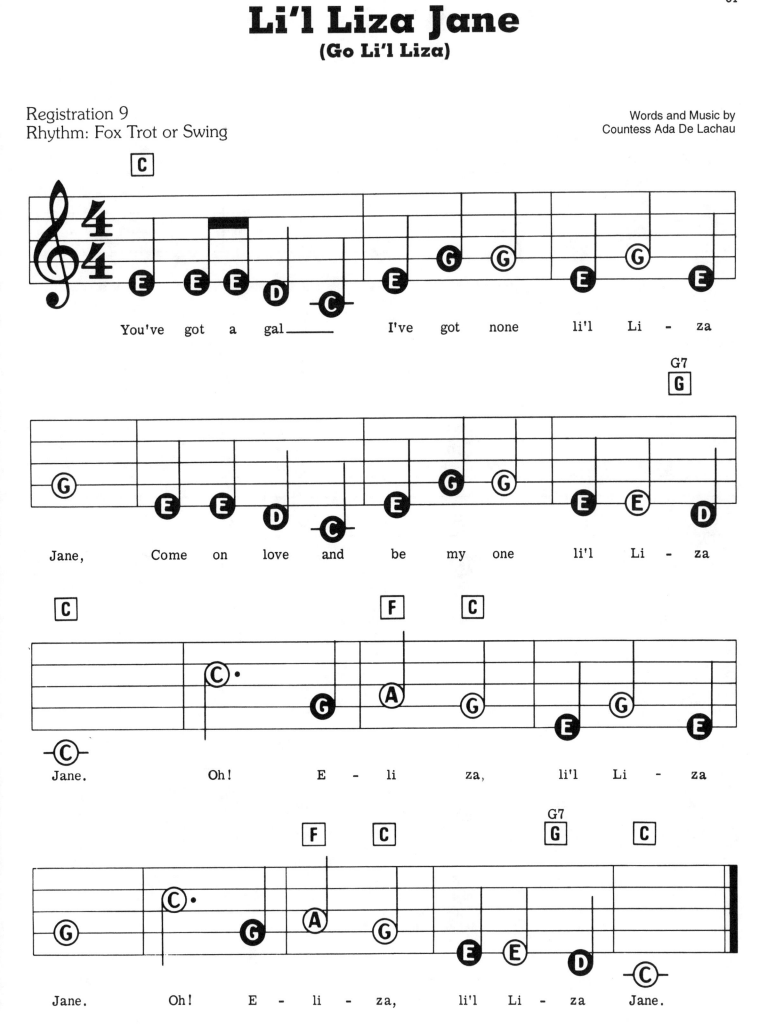

Jacob's Ladder

Registration 1
Rhythm: Waltz

African-American Spiritual

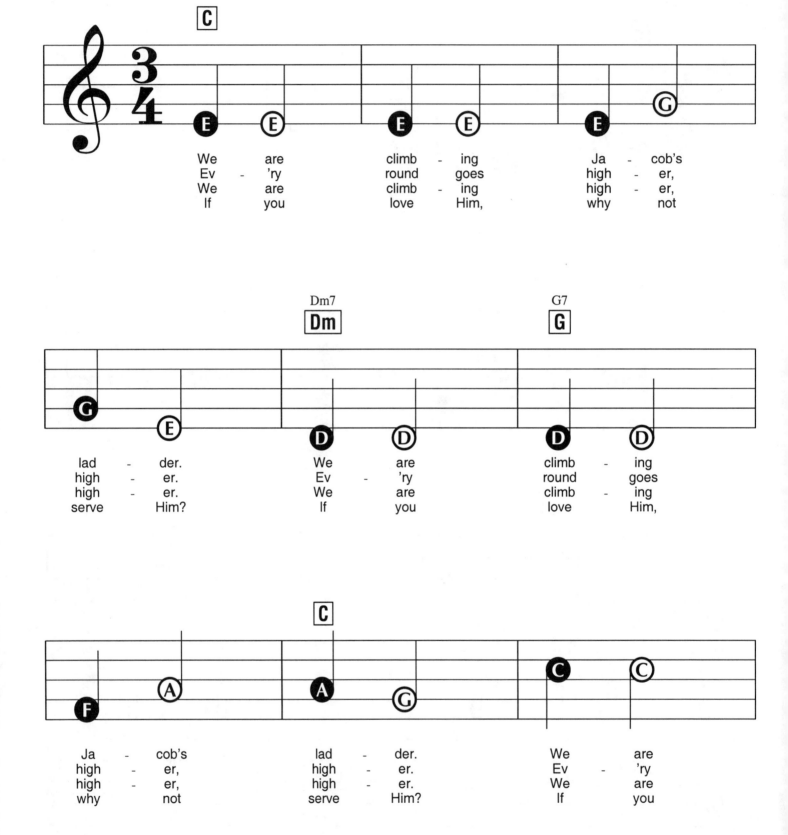

63

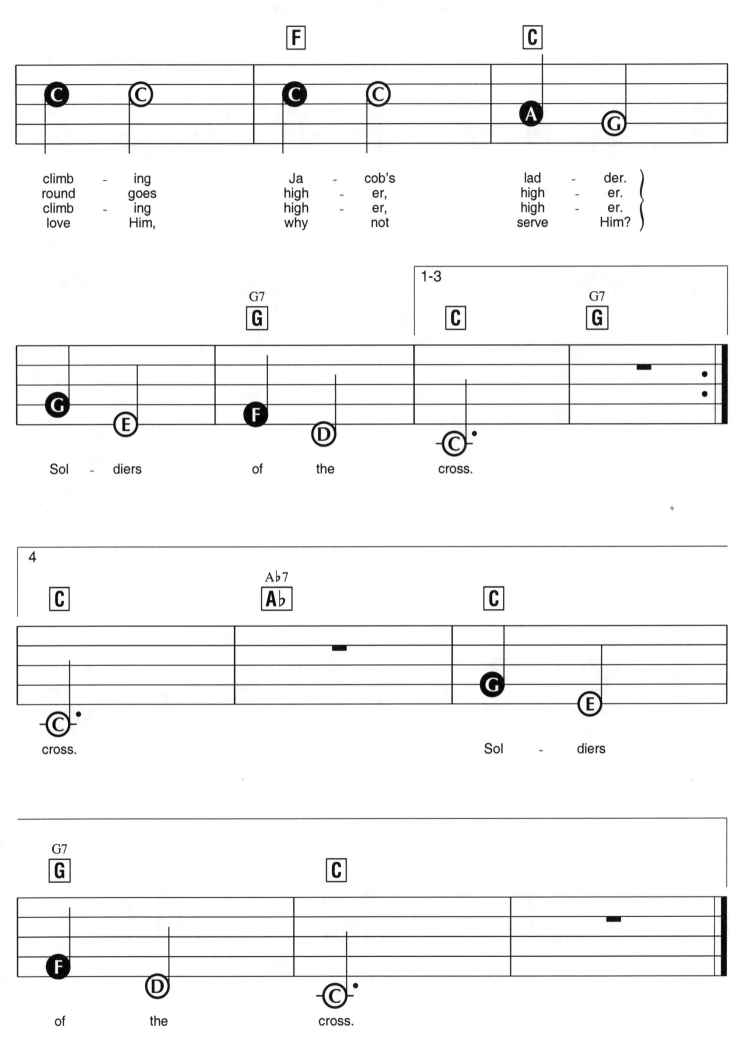

John Henry

Registration 1
Rhythm: Fox Trot or Ballad

West Virginia Folksong

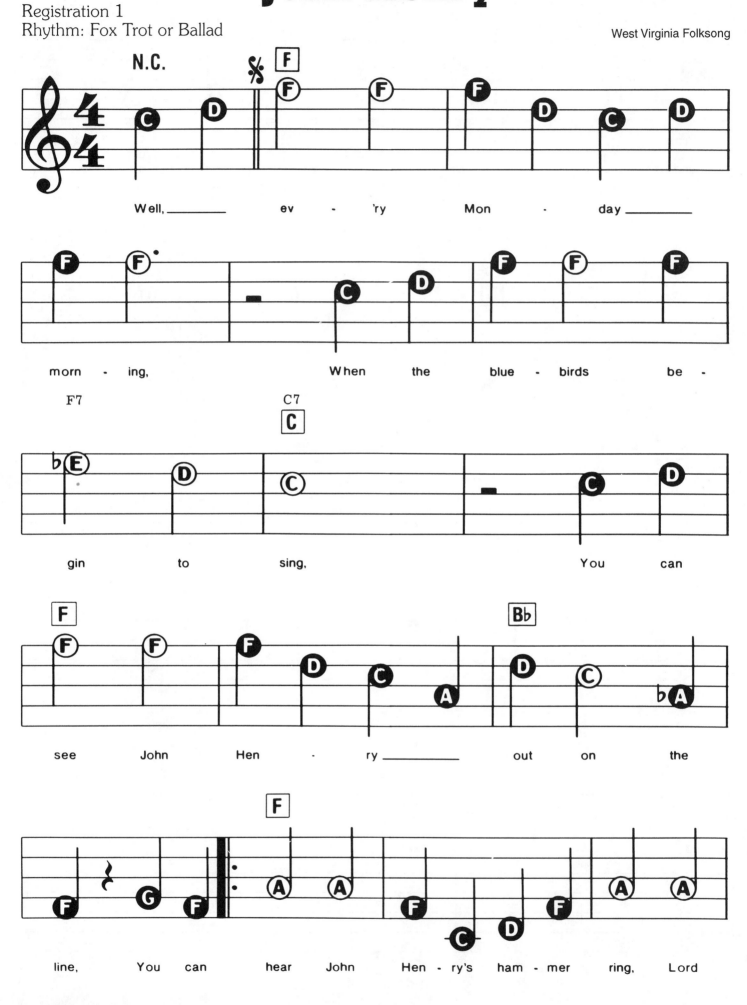

Last time to Coda ⊕

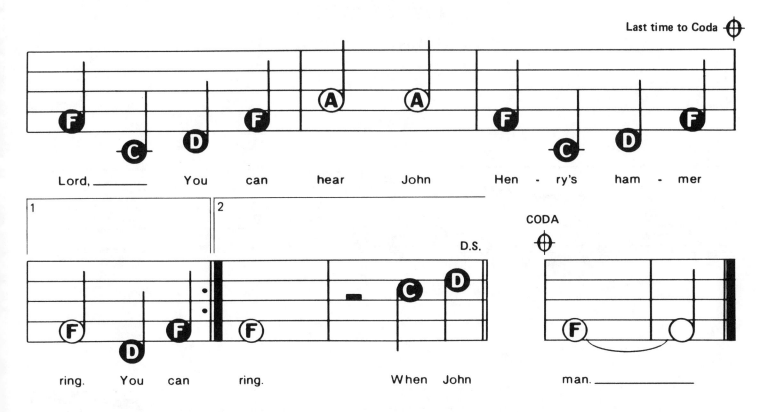

2. When John Henry was a little baby,
   A-sitting on his papa's knee,
   He picked up a hammer and a little
      piece of steel,
   Said, "Hammer's gonna be the death
      of me"... (Repeat)

3. Well, the captain said to John Henry,
   "Gonna bring me a steam drill 'round,
   Gonna bring me a steam drill out on
      the job,
   Gonna whup that steel on down"...
   (Repeat)

4. John Henry said to his captain,
   "A man ain't nothin' but a man,
   And before I let that steam drill beat
      me down,
   I'll die with a hammer in my hand"...
   (Repeat)

5. John Henry said to his shaker,
   "Shaker, why don't you pray?
   'Cause if I miss this little piece of steel,
   Tomorrow be your buryin' day"...
   (Repeat)

6. John Henry was driving on the mountain
   And his hammer was flashing fire.
   And the last words I heard that poor boy
      say,
   "Gimme a cool drink of water 'fore I
      die"... (Repeat)

7. John Henry, he drove fifteen feet,
   The steam drill only made nine.
   But he hammered so hard that he broke
      his poor heart,
   And he laid down his hammer and he
      died... (Repeat)

8. They took John Henry to the graveyard
   And they buried him in the sand.
   And every locomotive comes a-roaring
      by says,
   "There lies a steel-driving man"...
   (Repeat)

Joshua
(Fit the Battle of Jericho)

Registration 6
Rhythm: Swing

African-American Spiritual

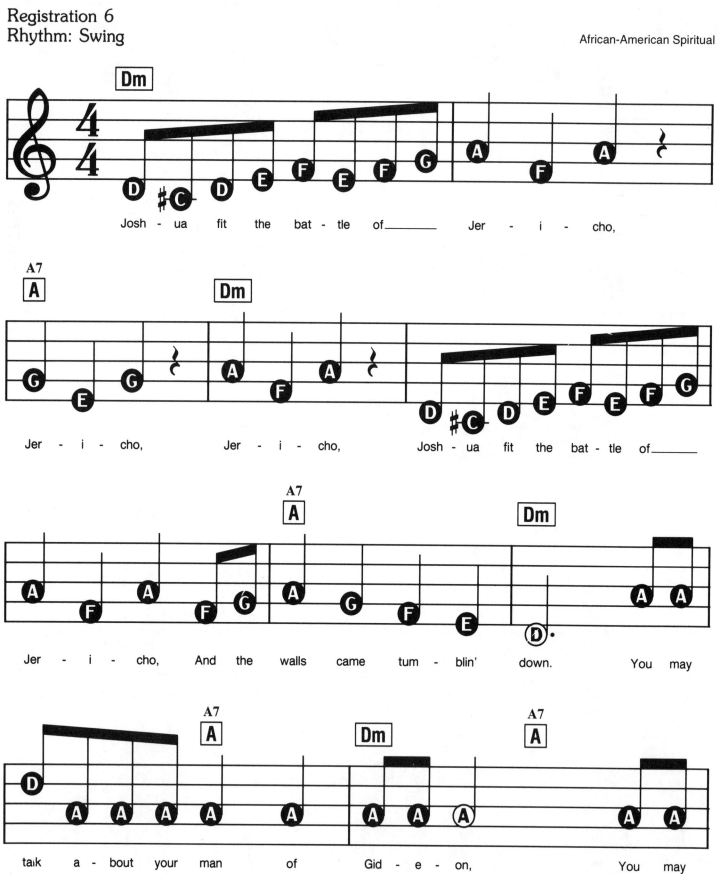

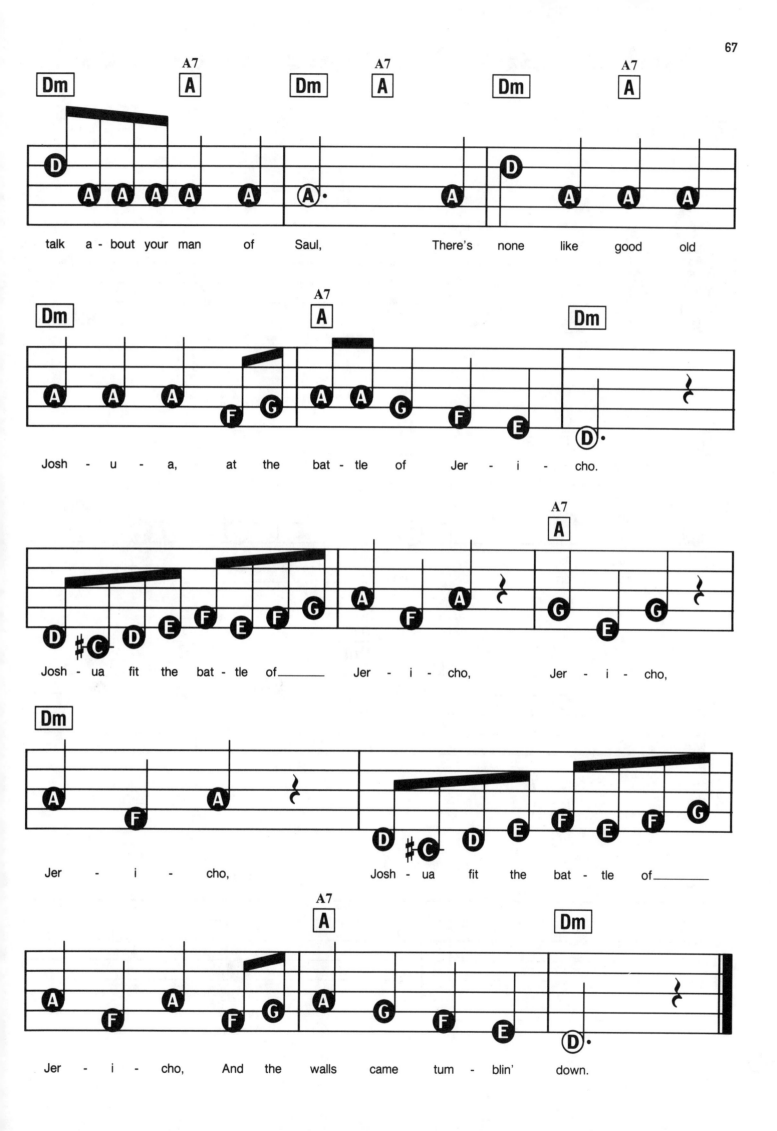

Let Us Break Bread Together

Registration 3
Rhythm: Pops

Traditional Spiritual

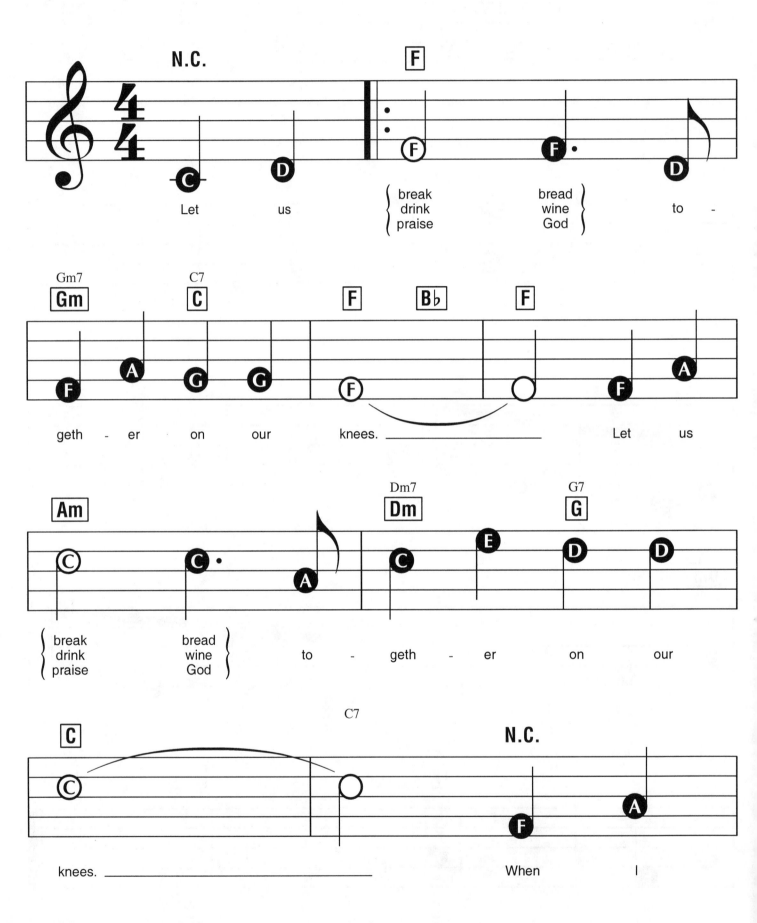

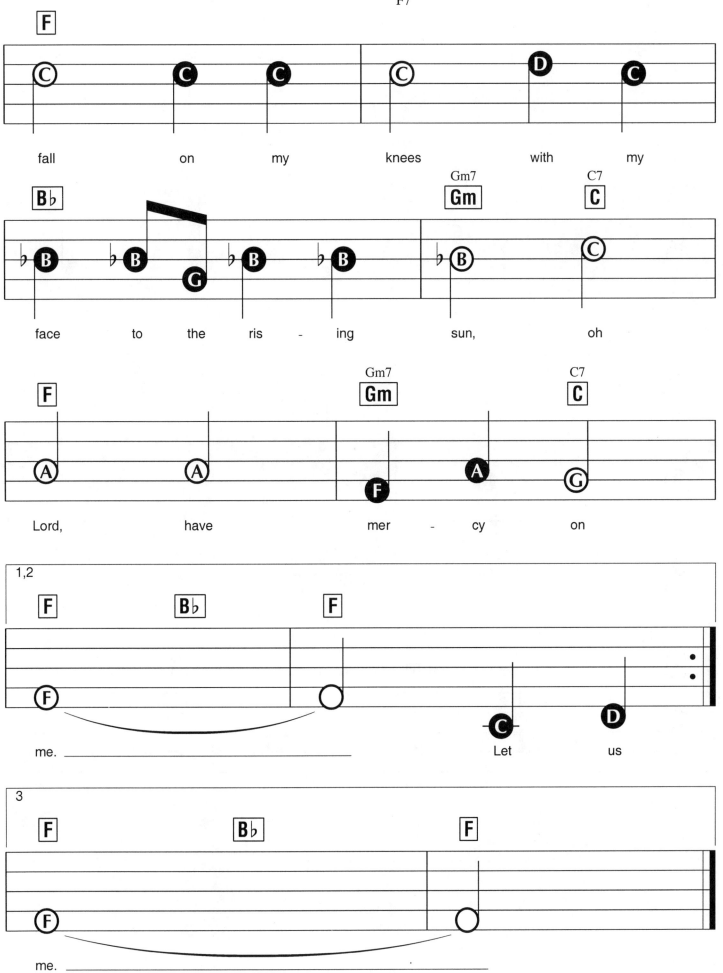

The Lonesome Road

Registration 8
Rhythm: Swing

African-American Spiritual

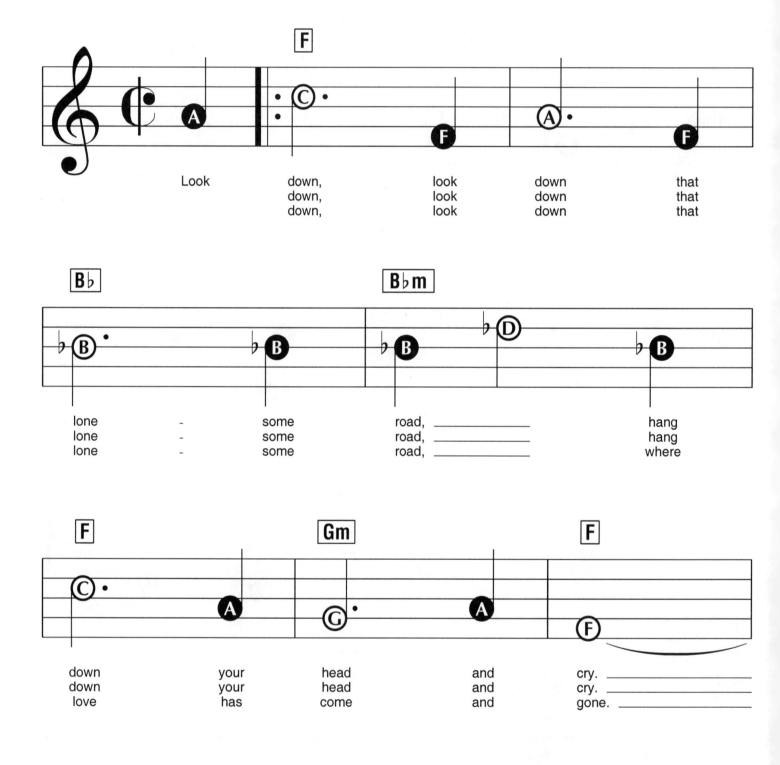

Look   down,   look   down   that
down,   look   down   that
down,   look   down   that

lone   -   some   road, _____   hang
lone   -   some   road, _____   hang
lone   -   some   road, _____   where

down   your   head   and   cry. _____
down   your   head   and   cry. _____
love   has   come   and   gone. _____

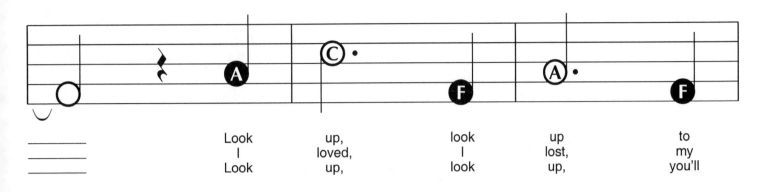

Look up, look up, to
Look up, look up, you'll

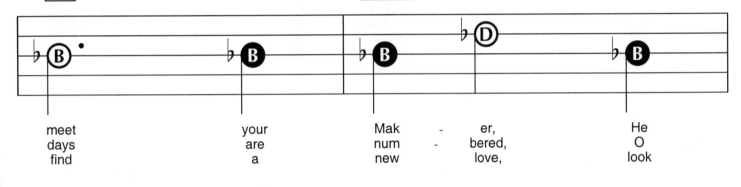

meet your Mak - er, He
days are num - bered, O
find a new love, look

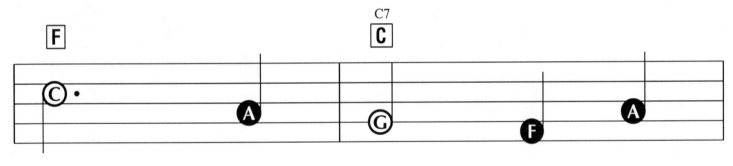

looks for you from on
Lord, I want to
up and keep trav - 'lin'

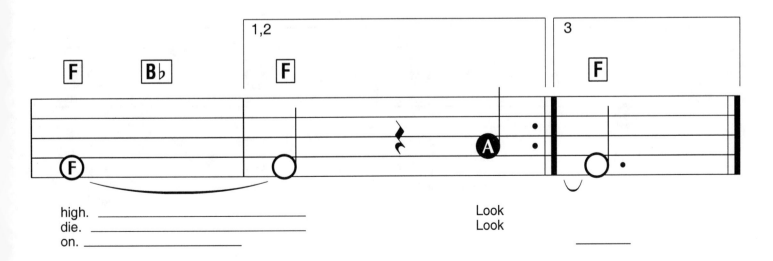

high.
die.
on.

Look
Look

Never Said a Mumblin' Word

Registration 9
Rhythm: Ballad

African-American Spiritual

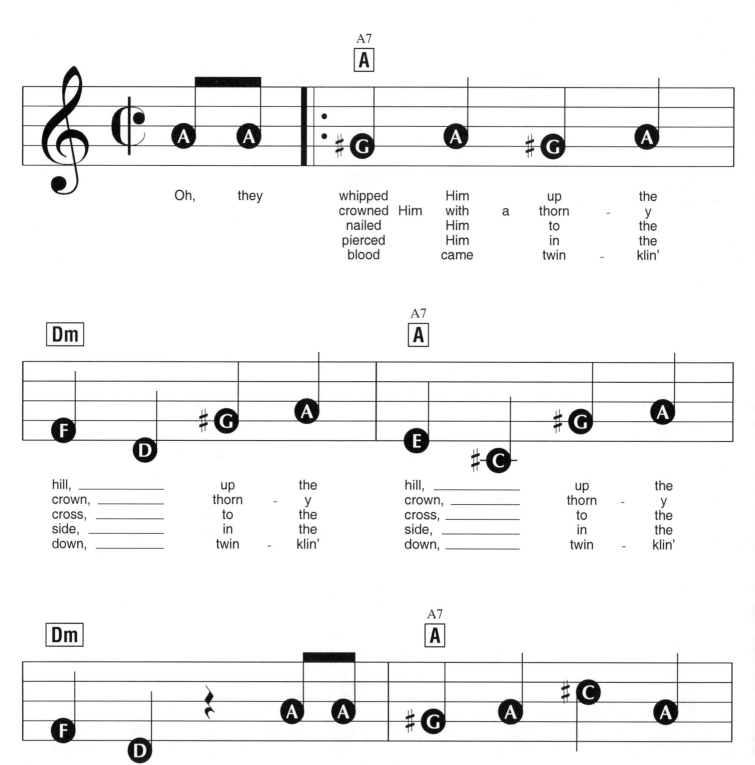

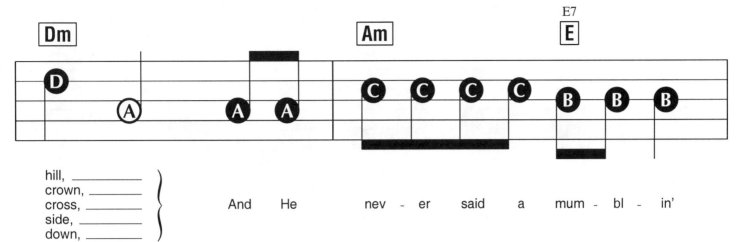

hill, _____
crown, _____
cross, _____
side, _____
down, _____

And He nev - er said a mum - bl - in'

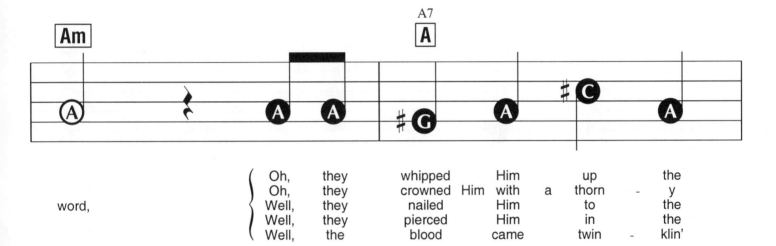

word,

Oh, they whipped Him up the
Oh, they crowned Him with a thorn - y
Well, they nailed Him to the
Well, they pierced Him in the
Well, the blood came twin - klin'

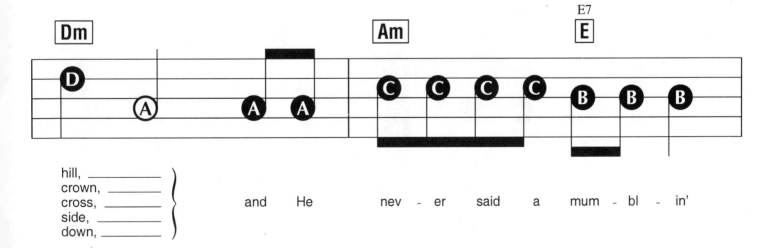

hill, _____
crown, _____
cross, _____
side, _____
down, _____

and He nev - er said a mum - bl - in'

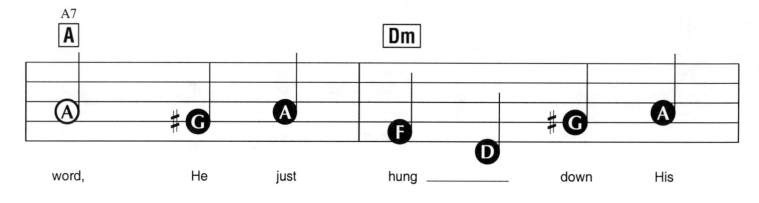

word,   He   just   hung _____ down   His

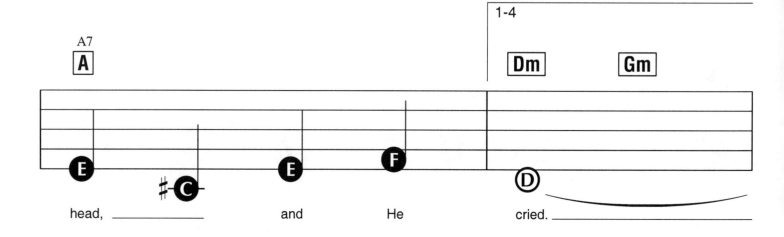

head, _____ and   He   cried. _____

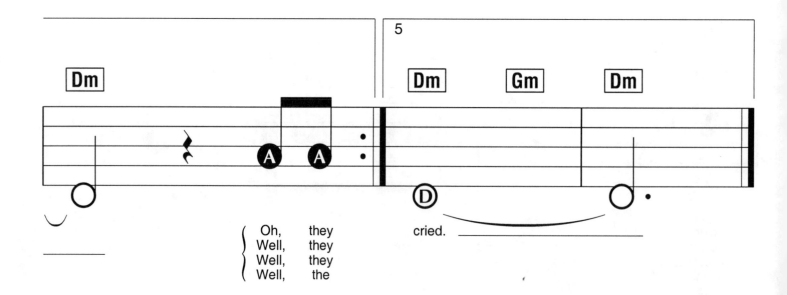

Oh,   they
Well,   they
Well,   they
Well,   the

cried. _____

Old Joe Clark

Registration 1
Rhythm: Country or Fox Trot

Tennessee Folksong

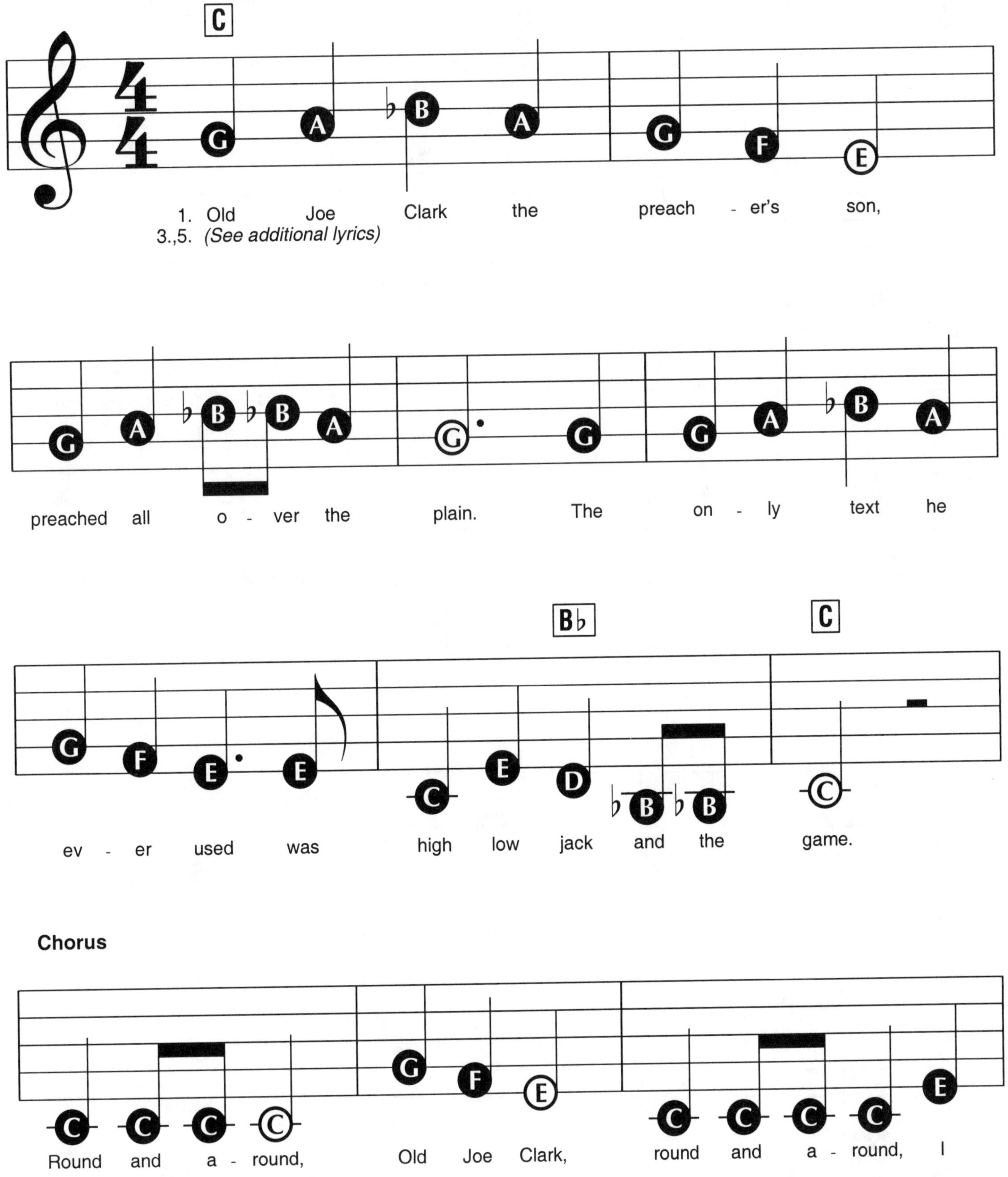

1. Old Joe Clark the preach - er's son,
3., 5. *(See additional lyrics)*

preached all o - ver the plain. The on - ly text he

ev - er used was high low jack and the game.

Chorus

Round and a - round, Old Joe Clark, round and a - round, I

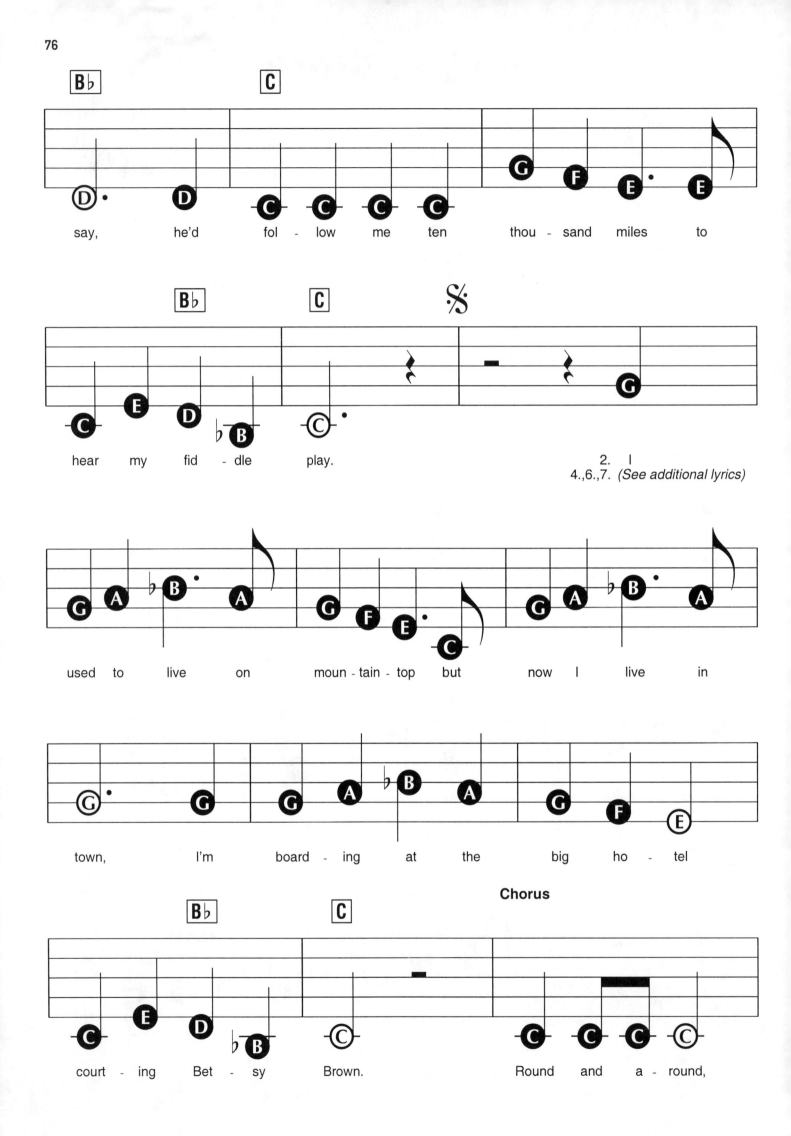

say, he'd fol - low me ten thou - sand miles to

hear my fid - dle play.

2. I
4.,6.,7. *(See additional lyrics)*

used to live on moun - tain - top but now I live in

town, I'm board - ing at the big ho - tel

Chorus

court - ing Bet - sy Brown. Round and a - round,

Additional Lyrics

3. When I was a little girl,
   I used to play with toys;
   Now I am a bigger girl,
   I'd rather play with boys. (Chorus)

4. When I was a little boy,
   I used to want a knife;
   Now I am a bigger boy,
   I only want a wife. (Chorus)

5. Wish I was a sugar tree,
   Standin' in the middle of some town;
   Ev'ry time a pretty girl passed,
   I'd shake some sugar down. (Chorus)

6. Old Joe had a yellow cat,
   She would not sing or pray;
   She stuck her head in a buttermilk jar
   And washed her sins away. (Chorus)

7. I wish I had a sweetheart;
   I'd set her on the shelf,
   And ev'ry time she'd smile at me
   I'd get up there myself. (Chorus)

Nobody Knows
the Trouble I've Seen

Registration 6
Rhythm: Fox Trot or Swing

African-American Spiritual

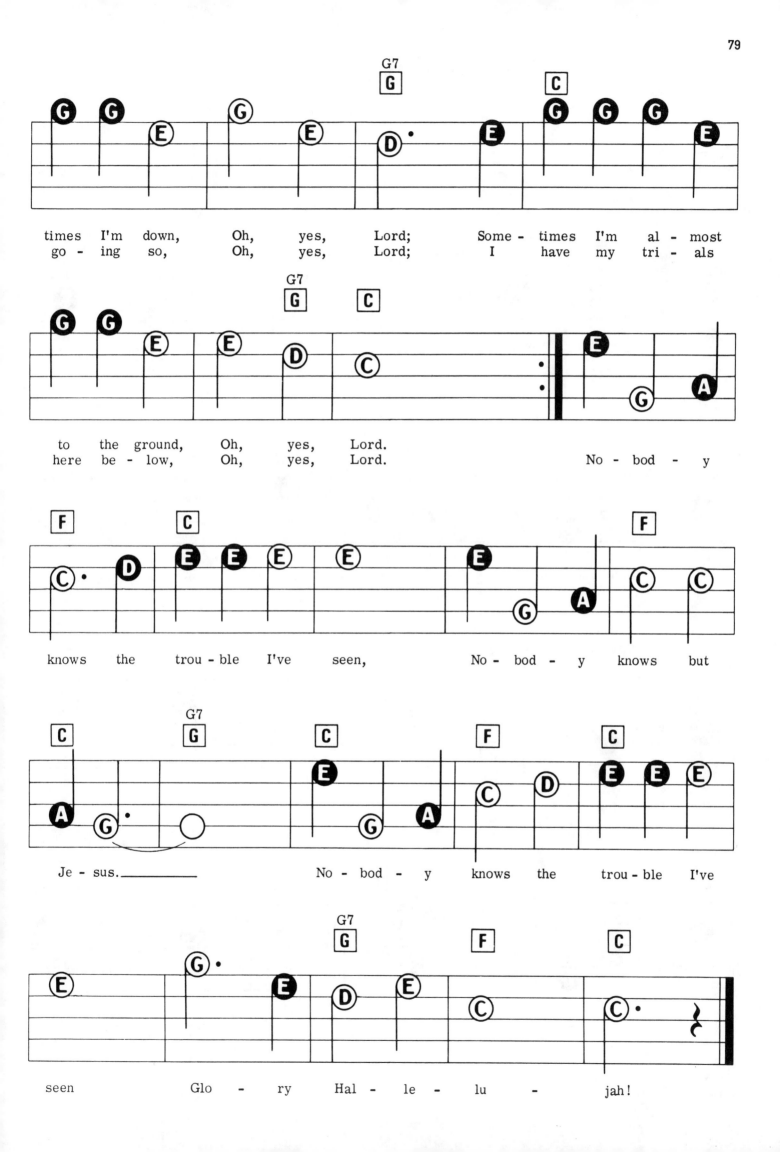

Oh! Susanna

Registration 3
Rhythm: Fox Trot

Words and Music by
Stephen C. Foster

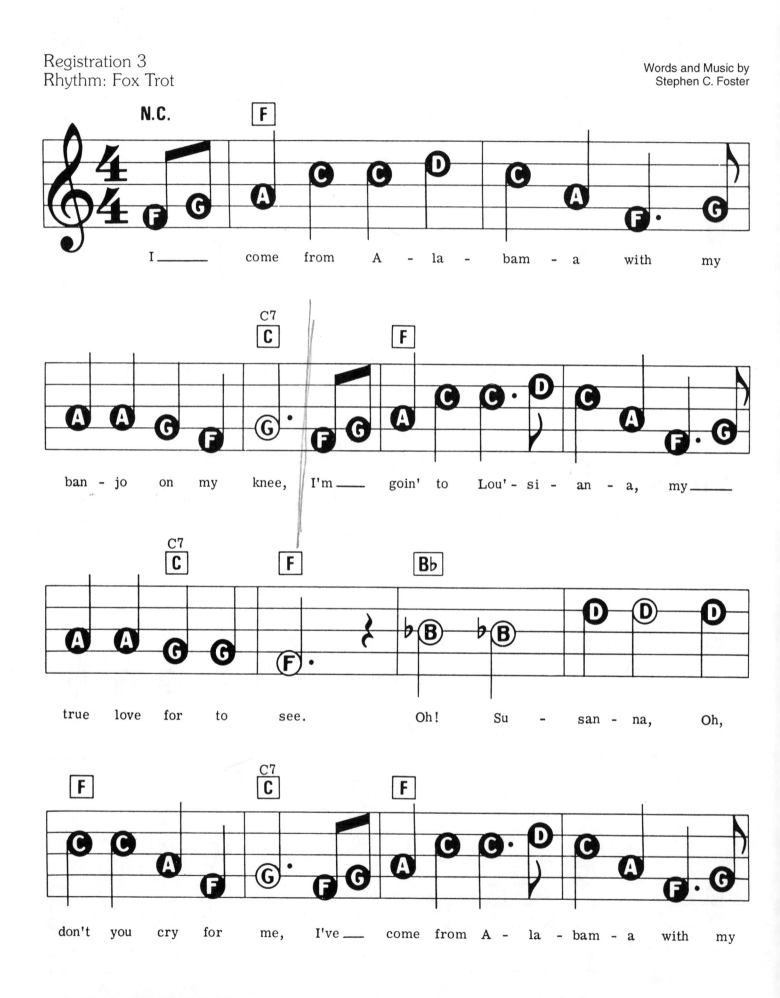

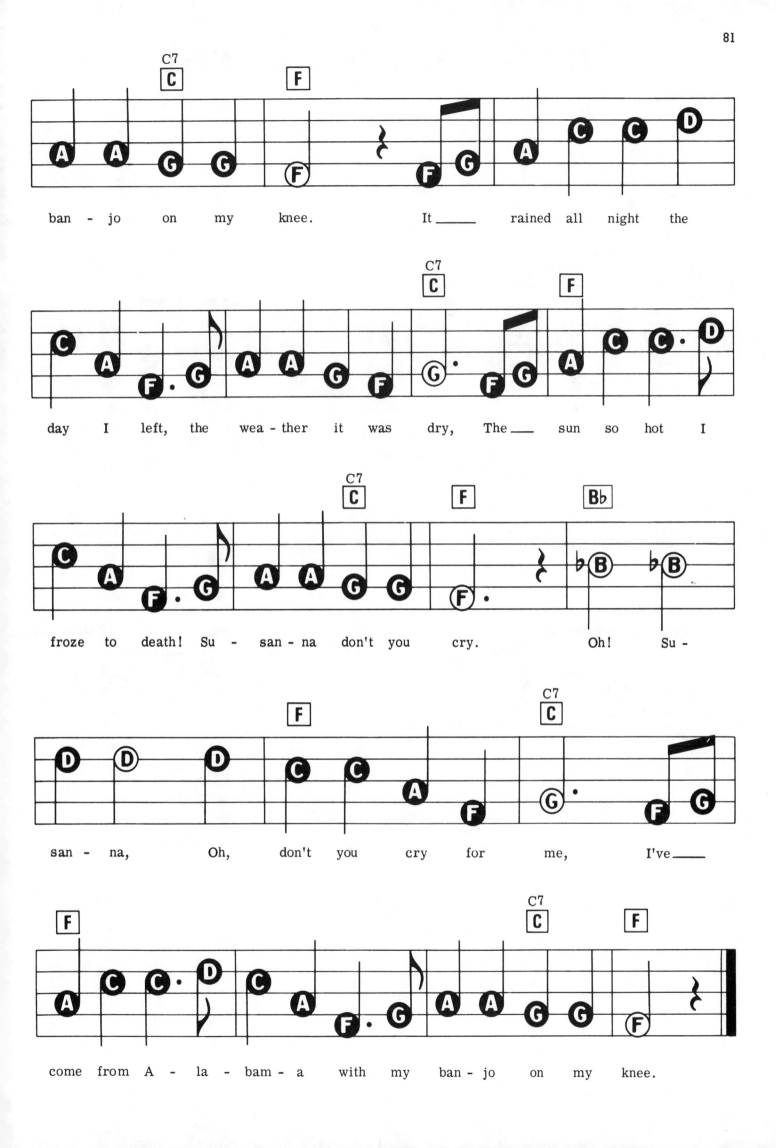

The Old Chisholm Trail

Registration 8
Rhythm: Country or Fox Trot

Texas Cowboy Song

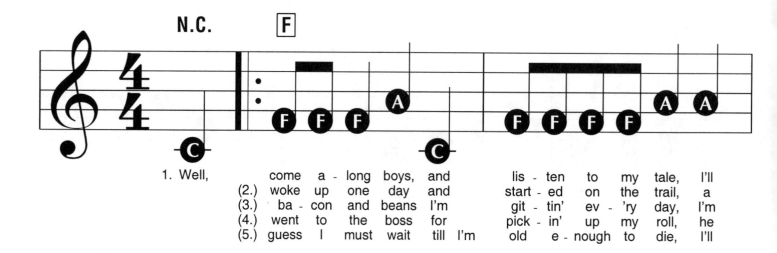

1. Well,   come a - long boys, and   lis - ten to my tale, I'll
(2.) woke up one day and   start - ed on the trail, a
(3.) ba - con and beans I'm   git - tin' ev - 'ry day, I'm
(4.) went to the boss for   pick - in' up my roll, he
(5.) guess I must wait till I'm   old e - nough to die, I'll

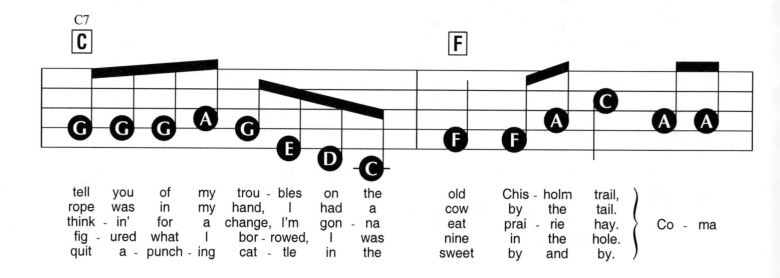

tell you of my trou - bles on the   old Chis - holm trail,
rope was in my hand, I had a   cow by the tail.
think - in' for a change, I'm gon - na   eat prai - rie hay.   } Co - ma
fig - ured what I bor - rowed, I was   nine in the hole.
quit a - punch - ing cat - tle in the   sweet by and by.

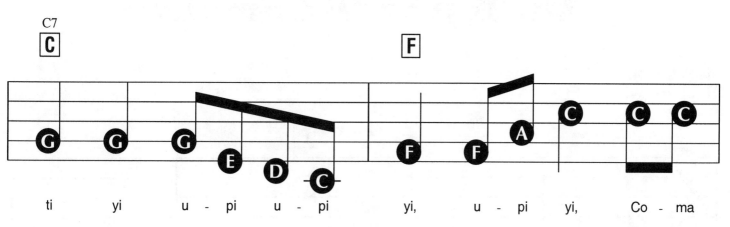

ti yi u – pi u – pi yi, u – pi yi, Co – ma

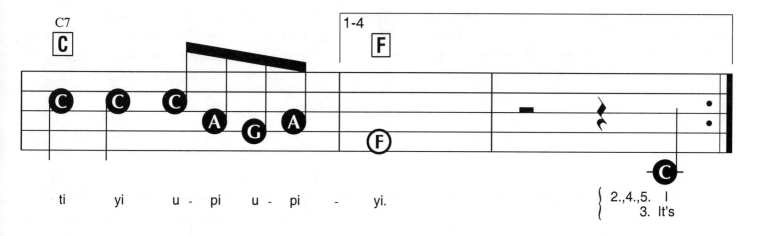

ti yi u – pi u – pi – yi.

{ 2.,4.,5. I
3. It's

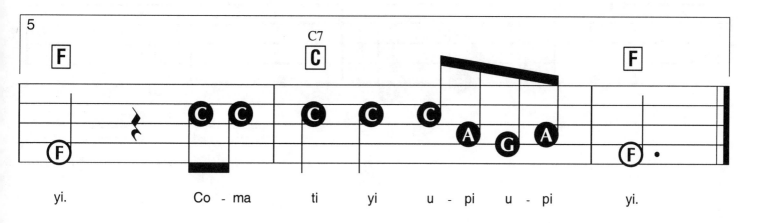

yi. Co – ma ti yi u – pi u – pi yi.

On Top of Ol' Smoky

Registration 1
Rhythm: Waltz

Kentucky Mountain Folksong

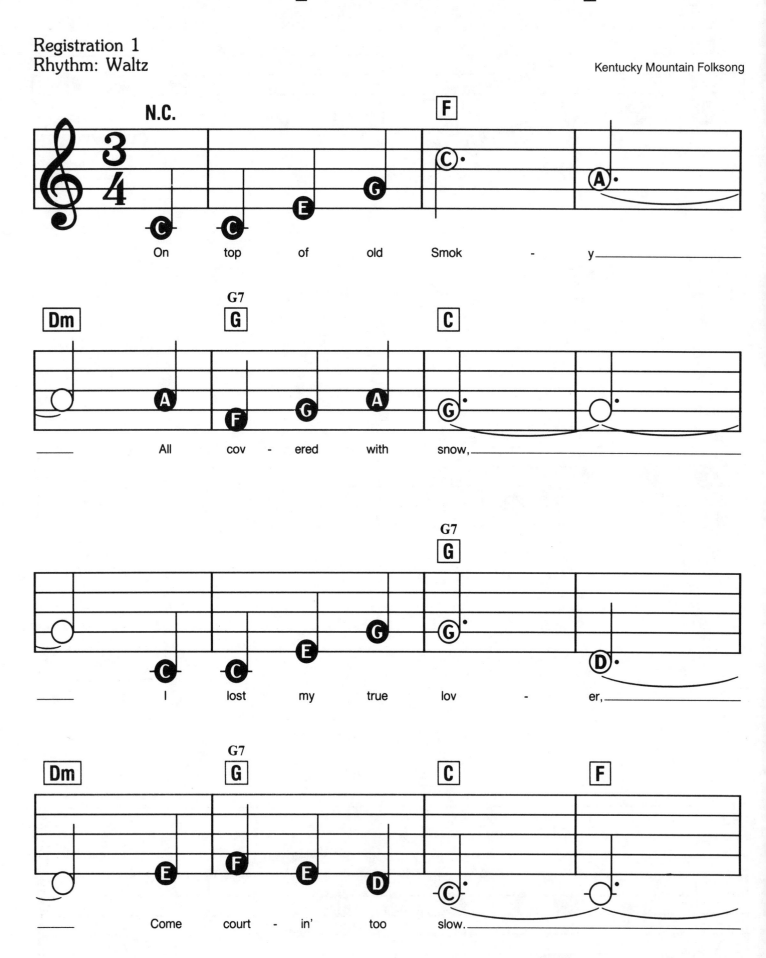

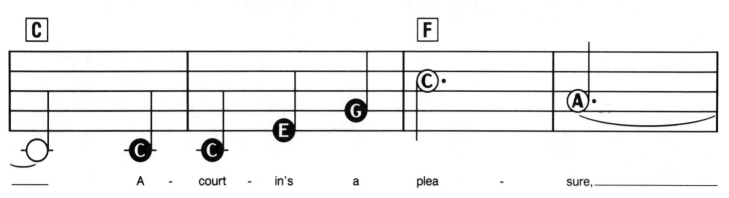
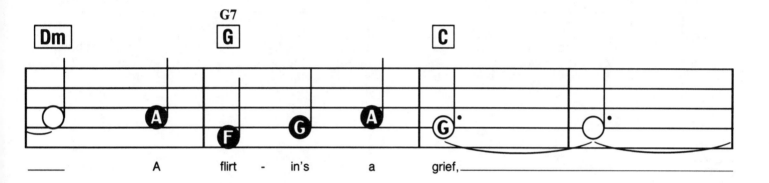
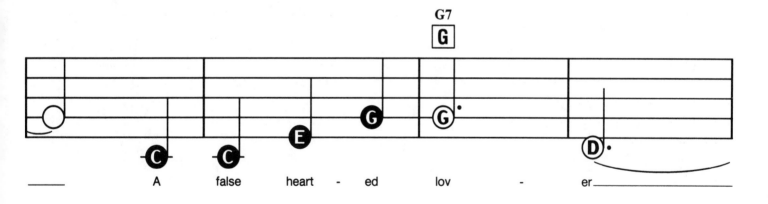
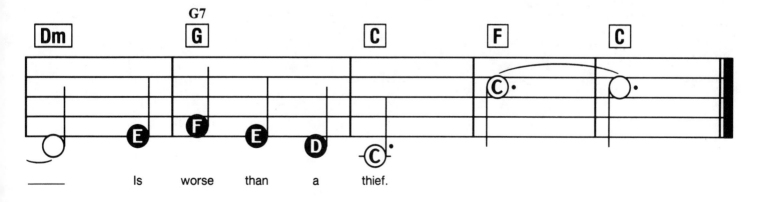

Once I Had a Sweetheart

Registration 4
Rhythm: Fox Trot

Southern Appalachian Folksong

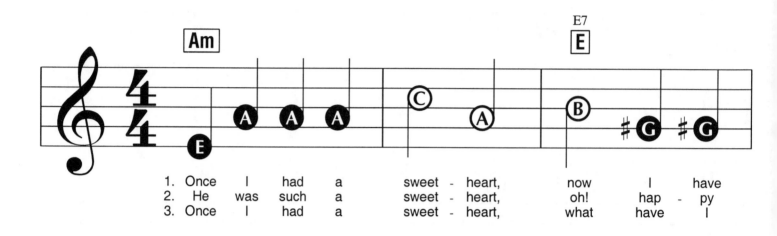

1. Once   I   had   a   sweet - heart,   now   I   have
2. He   was   such   a   sweet - heart,   oh!   hap - py
3. Once   I   had   a   sweet - heart,   what   have   I

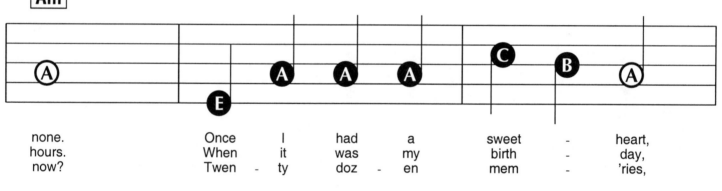

none.   Once   I   had   a   sweet - heart,
hours.   When   it   was   my   birth - day,
now?   Twen - ty   doz - en   mem - 'ries,

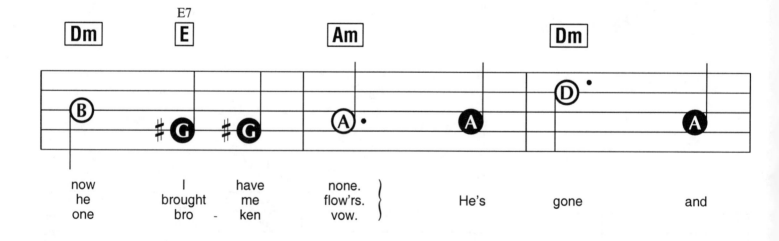

now   I   have   none.   ⎫
he   brought   me   flow'rs.   ⎬   He's   gone   and
one   bro - ken   vow.   ⎭

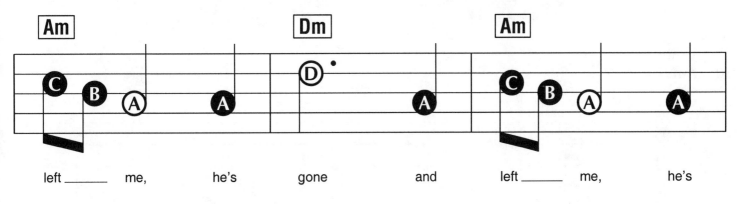

left _____ me, he's gone and left _____ me, he's

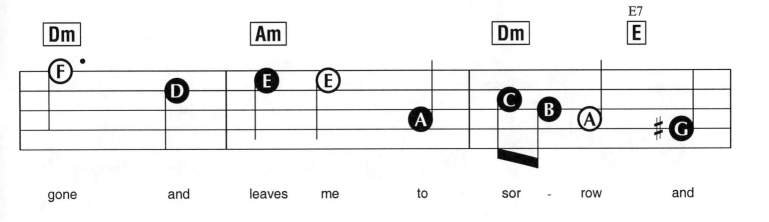

gone and leaves me to sor - row and

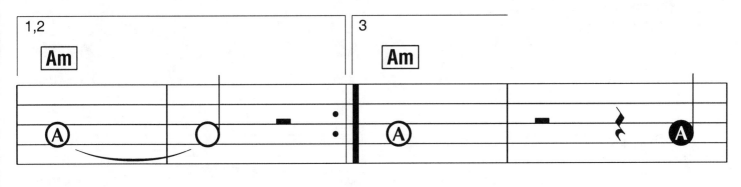

moan. _____ moan. And

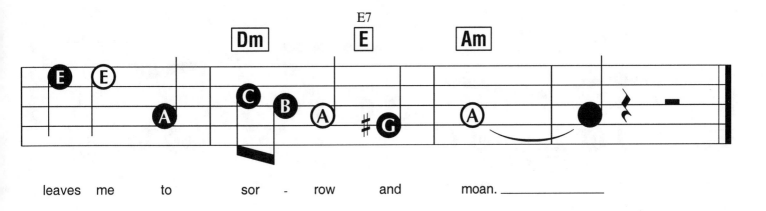

leaves me to sor - row and moan. _____

Polly Wolly Doodle

Registration 4
Rhythm: Rock or Swing

Traditional American Minstrel Song

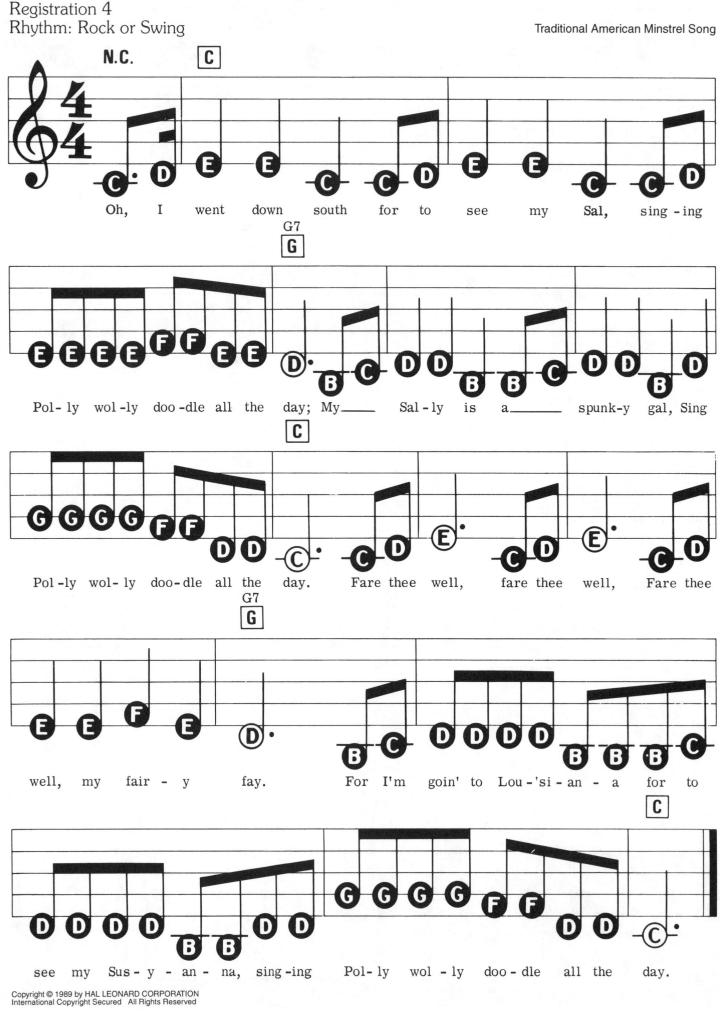

Rock-a-My Soul

Registration 9
Rhythm: Rock or 8 Beat

African-American Spiritual

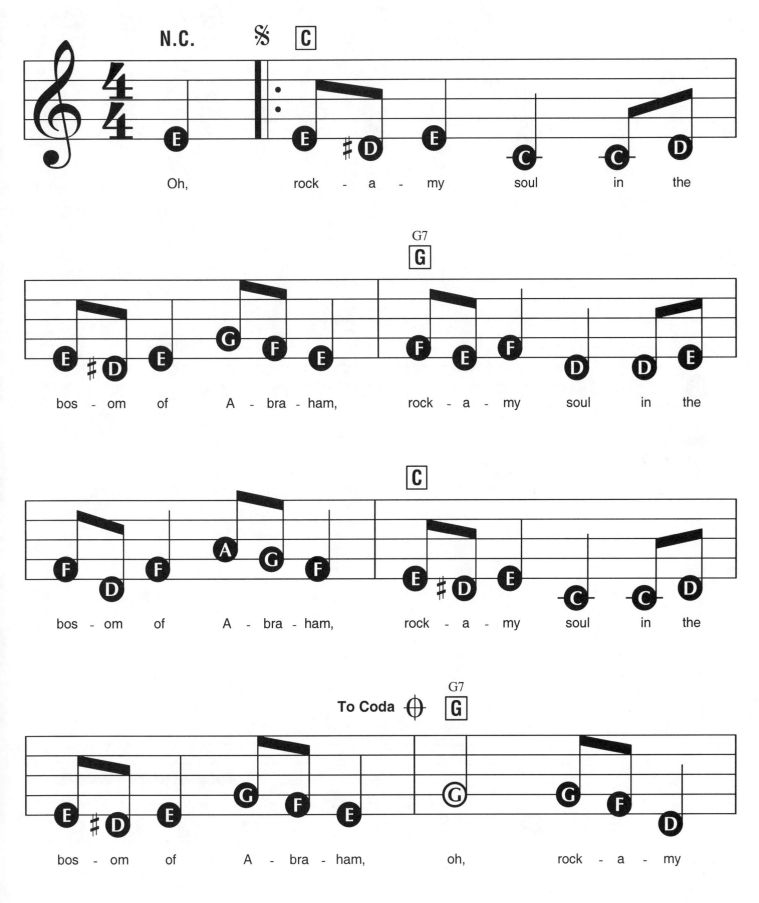

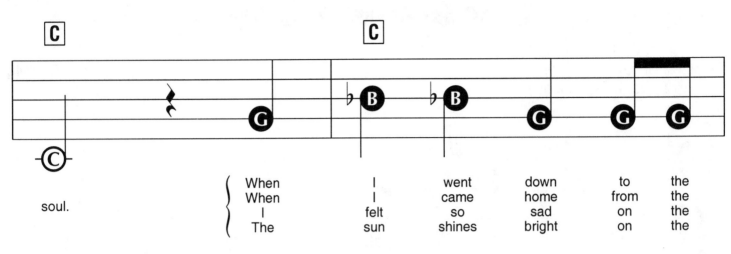

soul.

When	I	went	down	to	the
When	I	came	home	from	the
I	felt	so	sad	on	the
The	sun	shines	bright	on	the

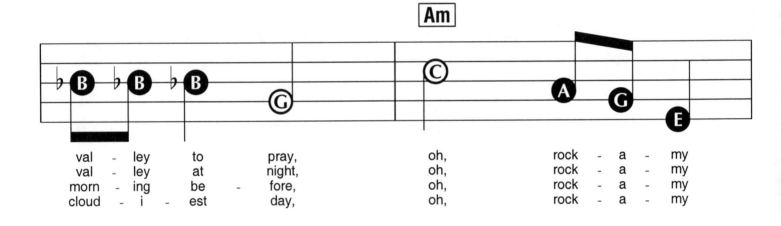

val - ley	to	pray,	oh,	rock - a - my
val - ley	at	night,	oh,	rock - a - my
morn - ing	be - fore,	oh,	rock - a - my
cloud - i - est	day,	oh,	rock - a - my

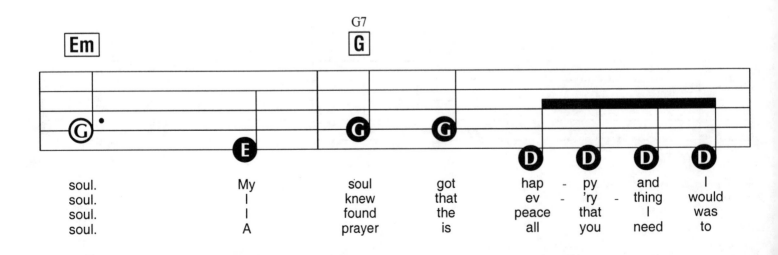

soul.	My	soul	got	hap - py	and	I
soul.	I	knew	that	ev - 'ry - thing	would
soul.	I	found	the	peace	that I	was
soul.	A	prayer	is	all	you	need	to

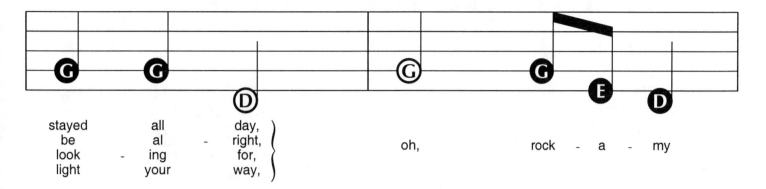

stayed   all   day,   oh,   rock - a - my
be   al -   right,
look -   ing   for,
light   your   way,

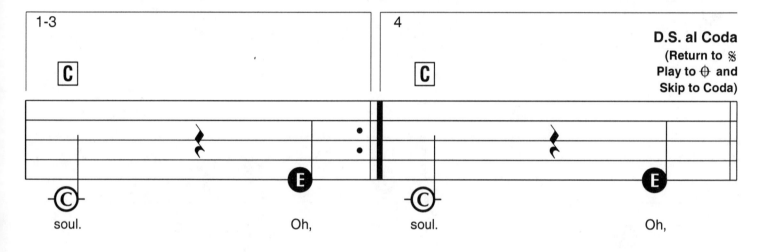

1-3

C

soul.   Oh,

4

C

D.S. al Coda
(Return to 𝄋
Play to ⊕ and
Skip to Coda)

soul.   Oh,

CODA G7
⊕ G

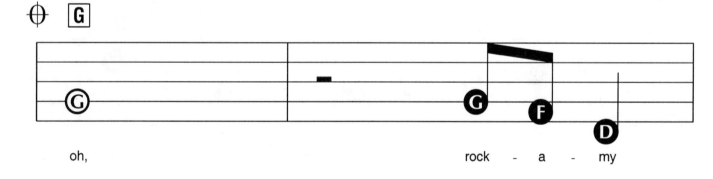

oh,   rock - a - my

C

soul!

The Red River Valley

Registration 4
Rhythm: Swing

Traditional American Cowboy Song

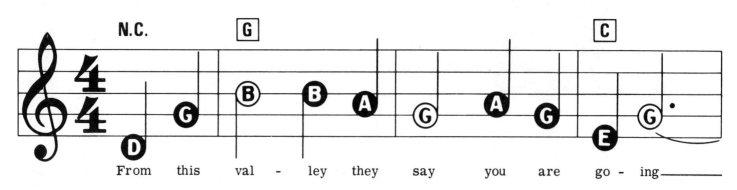

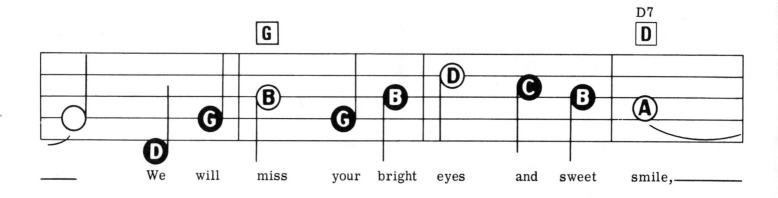

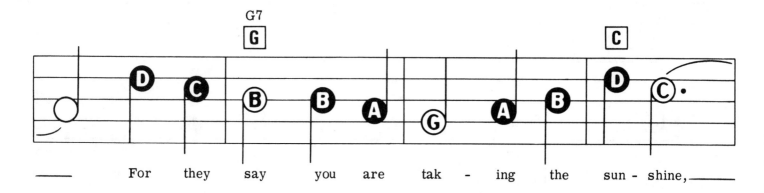

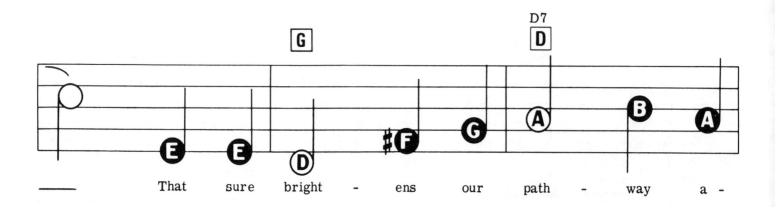

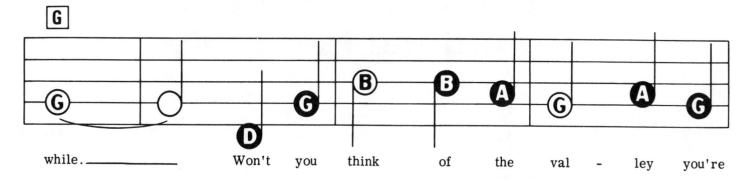

while._____ Won't you think of the val - ley you're

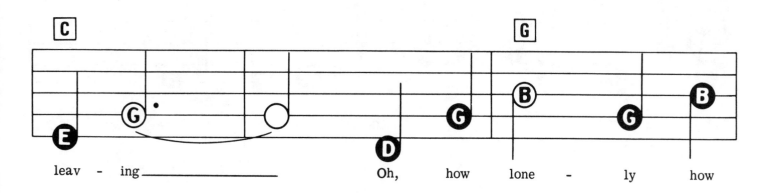

leav - ing_____ Oh, how lone - ly how

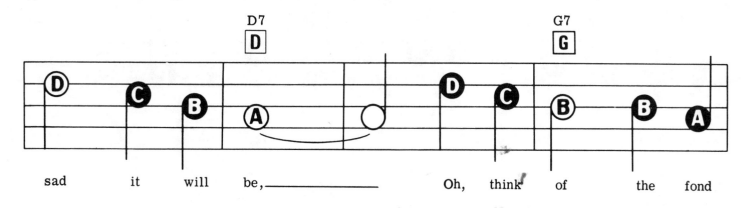

sad it will be,_____ Oh, think of the fond

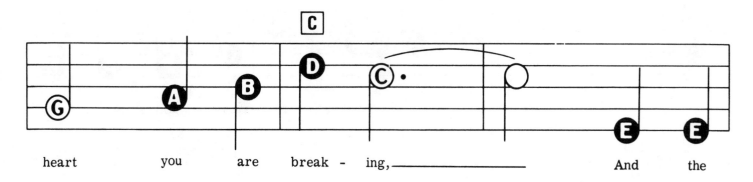

heart you are break - ing,_____ And the

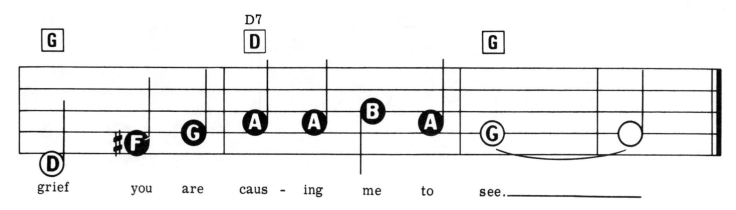

grief you are caus - ing me to see._____

She'll Be Comin' 'Round the Mountain

Registration 8
Rhythm: Fox Trot

Traditional

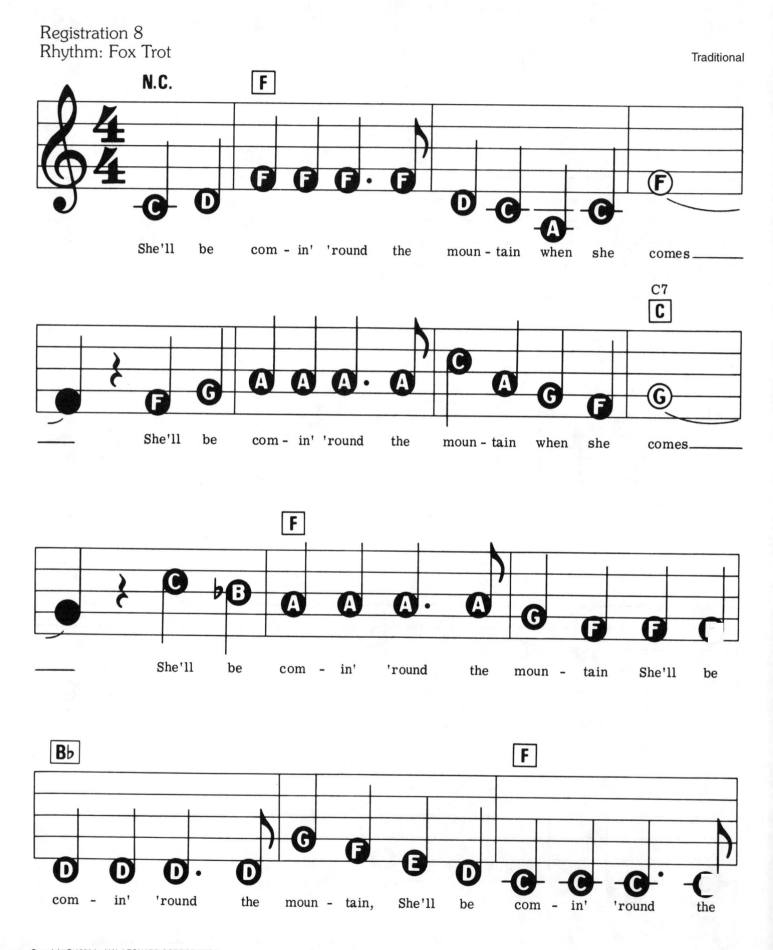

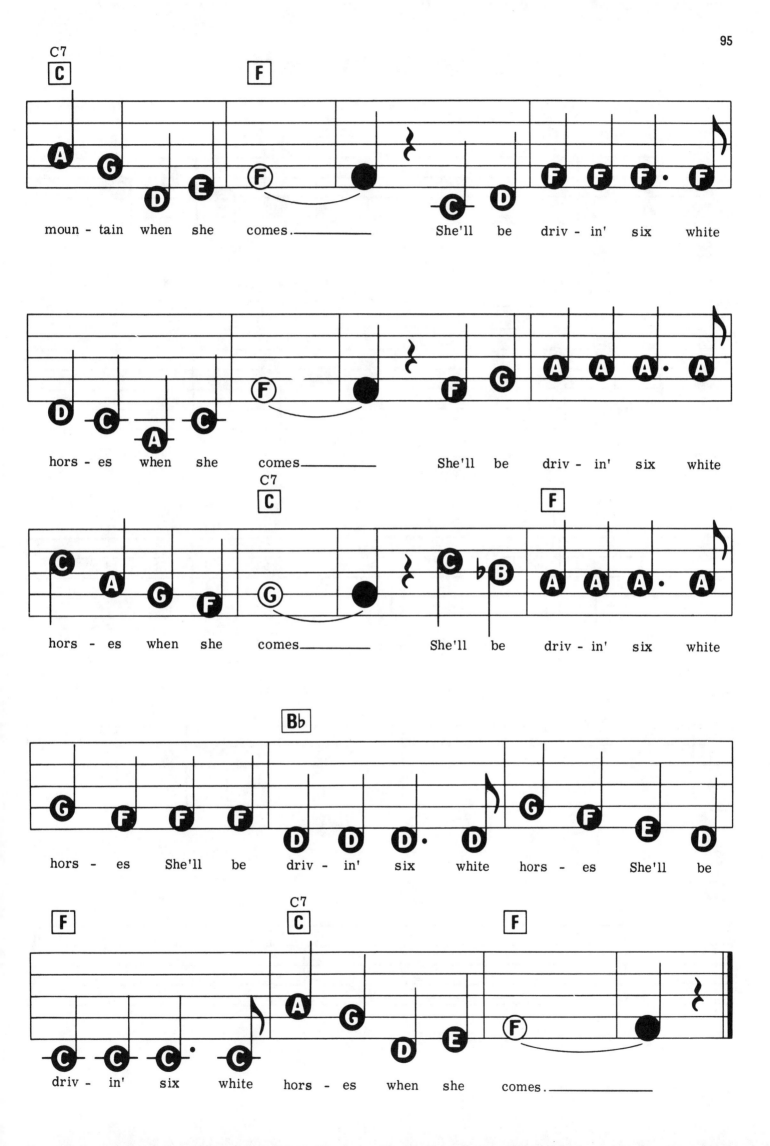

Shenandoah

Registration 3
Rhythm: Rock or Pops

American Folksong

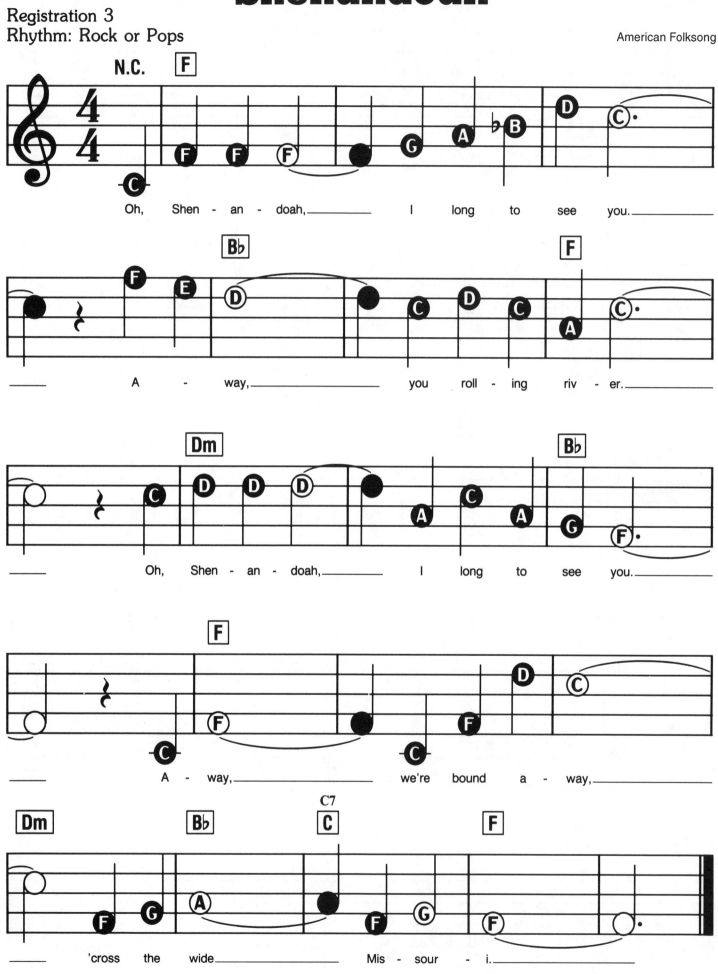

Shortnin' Bread

Registration 8
Rhythm: Country or Shuffle

Plantation Song

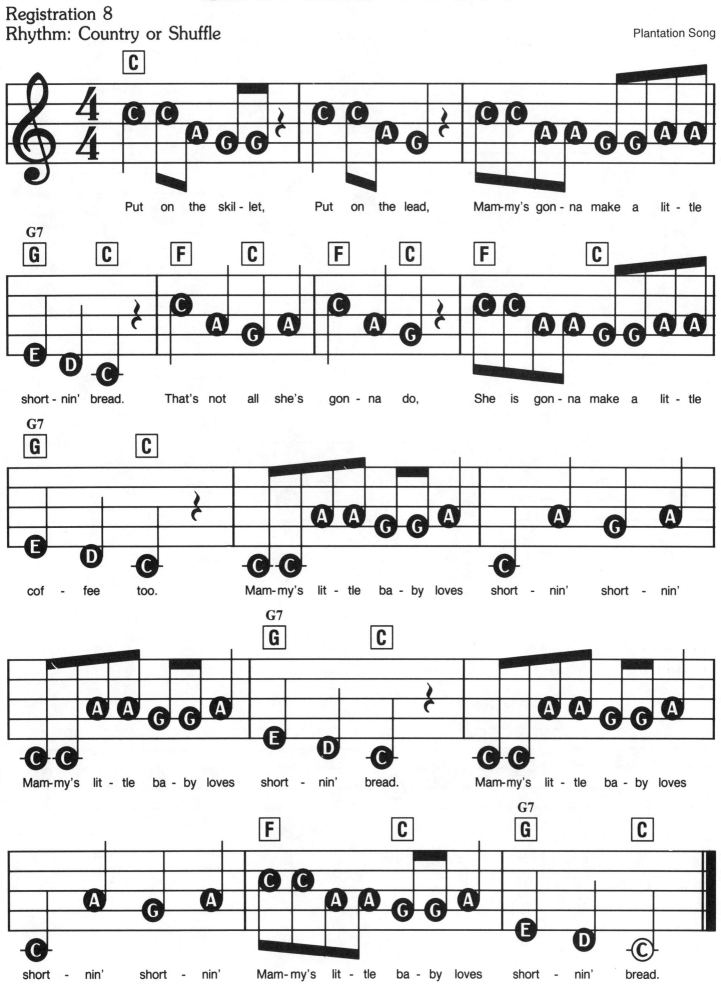

Shoo Fly, Don't Bother Me

Registration 9
Rhythm: Country or Fox Trot

Words by Billy Reeves
Music by Frank Campbell

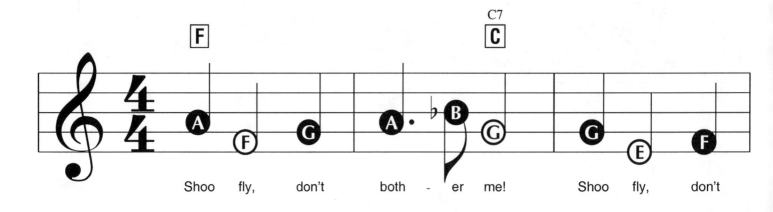

Shoo fly, don't both - er me! Shoo fly, don't

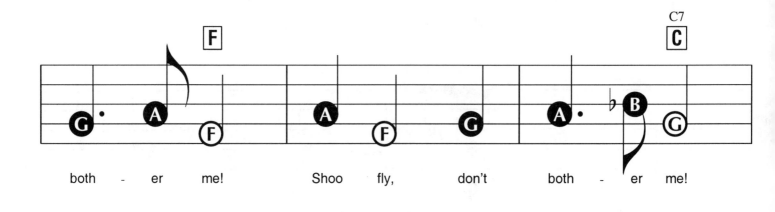

both - er me! Shoo fly, don't both - er me!

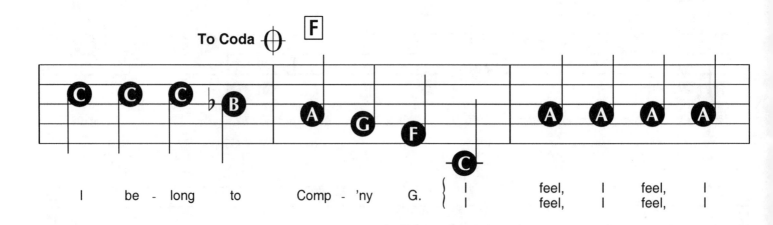

I be - long to Comp - 'ny G. { I feel, I feel, I
{ I feel, I feel, I

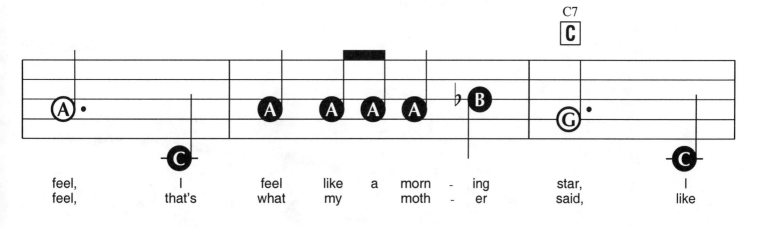

feel, I feel like a morn - ing star, I
feel, that's feel what like my a moth morn - er ing said, like

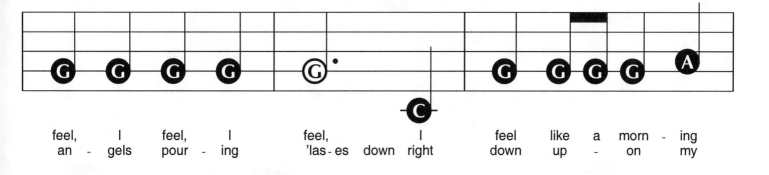

feel, I feel, I feel, I feel like a morn - ing
an - gels pour - ing 'las - es down right down up - on my

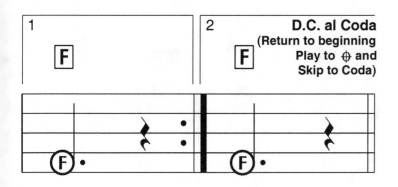

1 **F**

star.

2 **F** **D.C. al Coda**
(Return to beginning
Play to ⊕ and
Skip to Coda)

head.

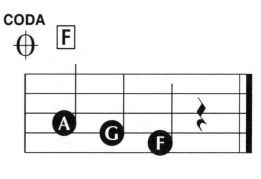

CODA ⊕ **F**

Comp - n'y G!

Simple Gifts

Registration 8
Rhythm: Fox Trot

Traditional Shaker Hymn

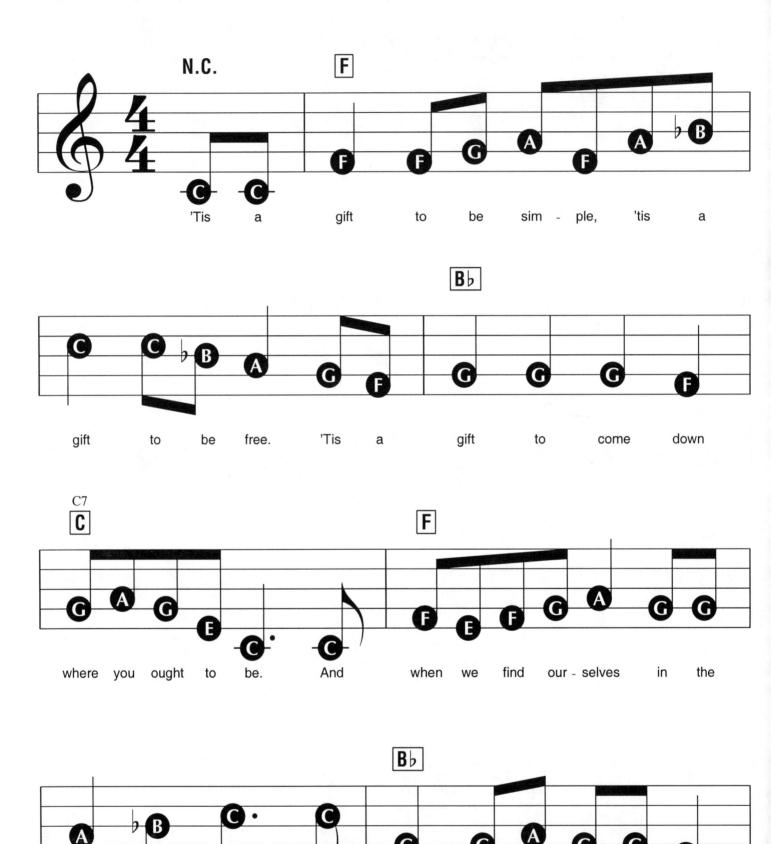

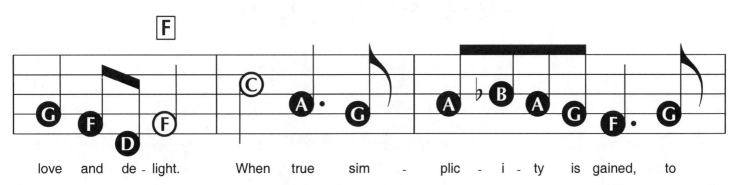

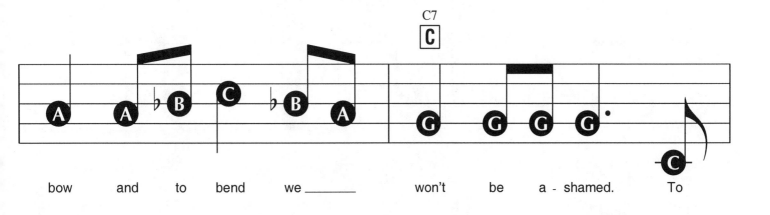

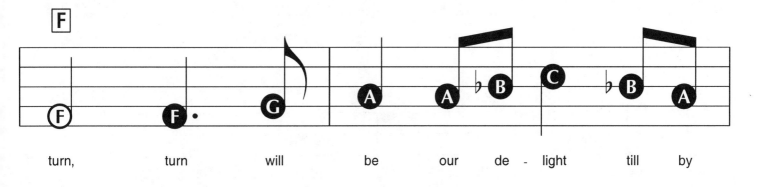

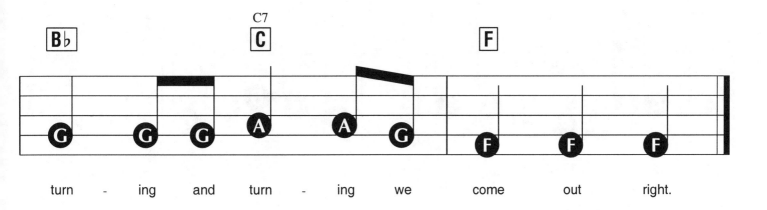

101

Skip to My Lou

Registration 10
Rhythm: Fox Trot

Traditional

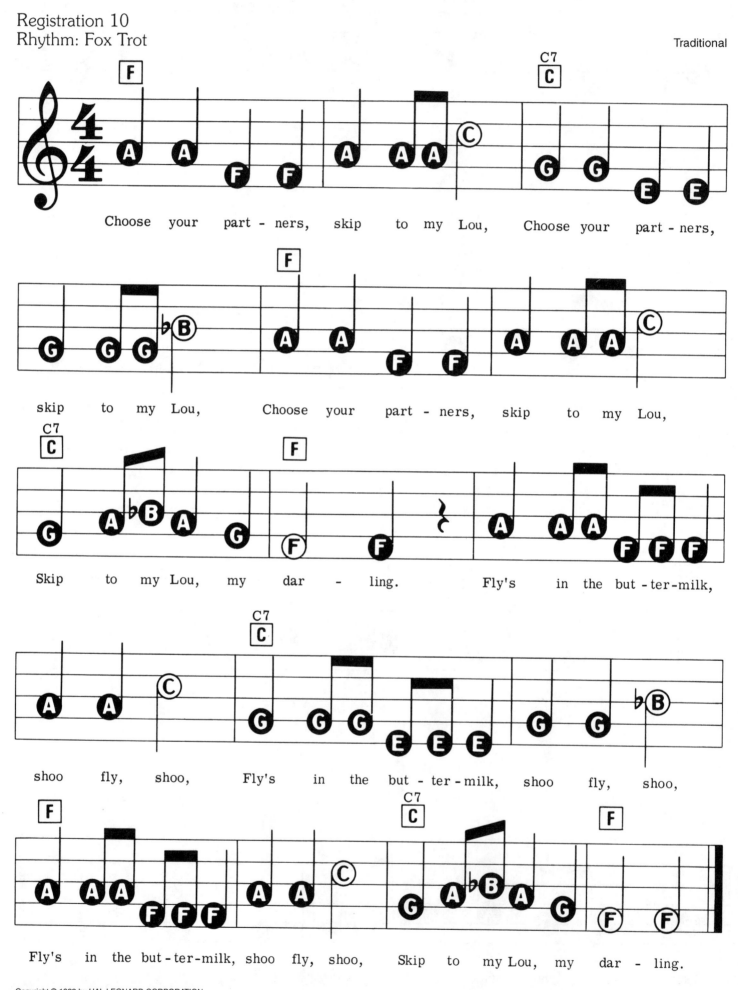

Somebody's Knockin' at Your Door

Registration 5
Rhythm: Fox Trot

African-American Spiritual

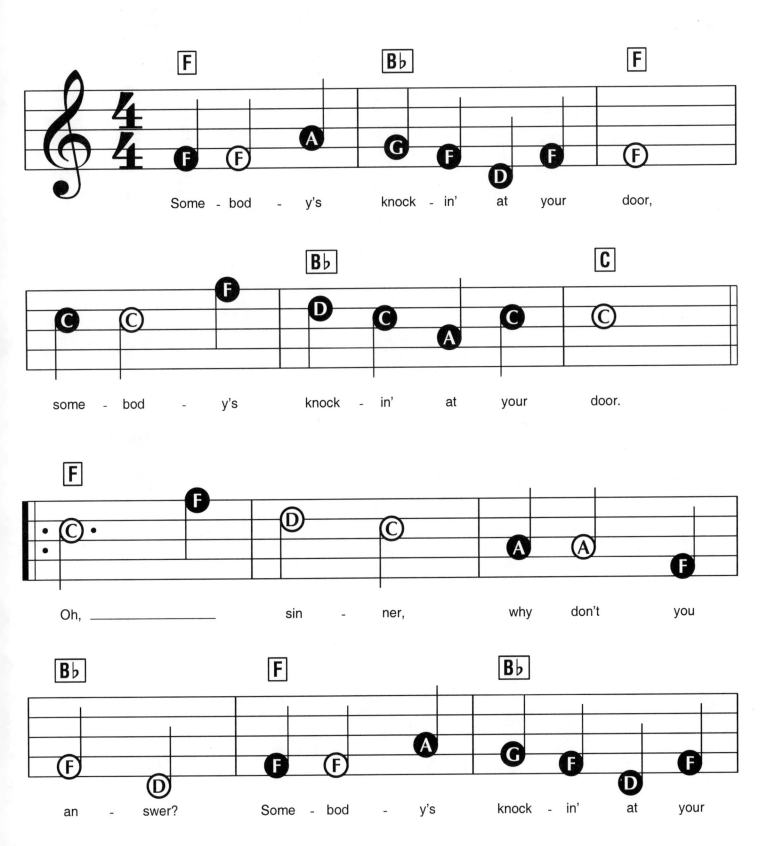

104

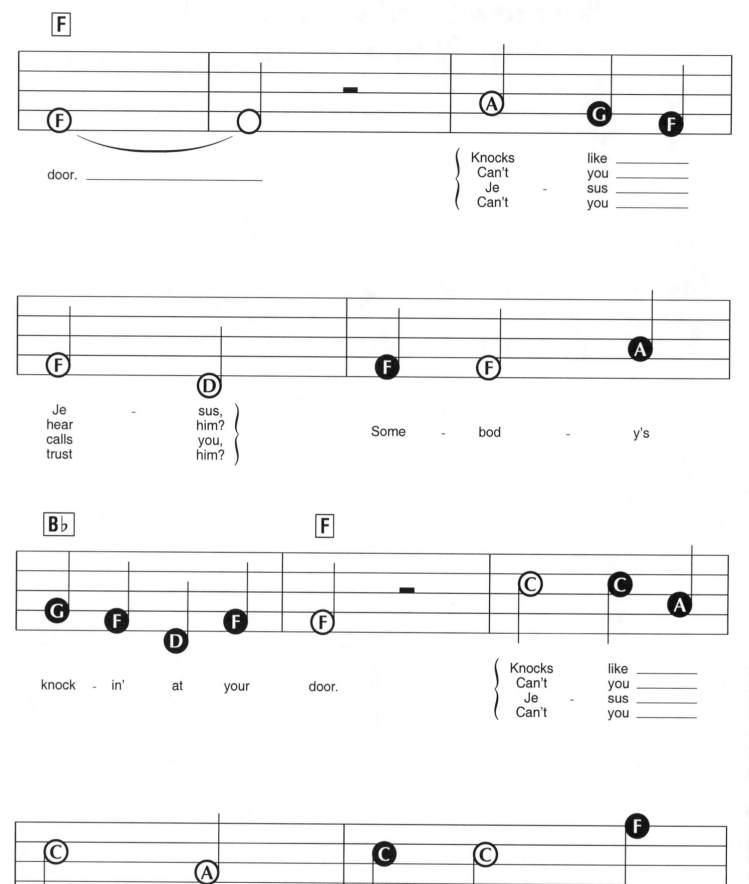

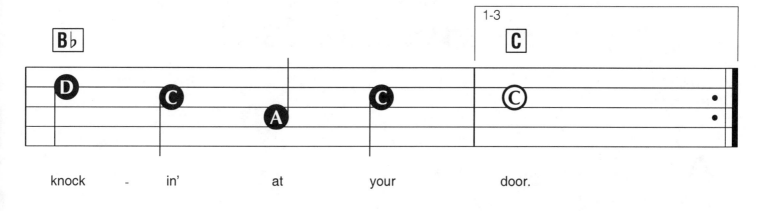

knock - in'   at   your   door.

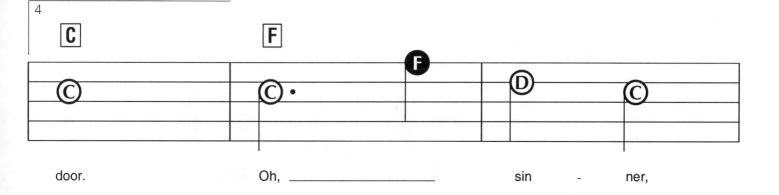

door.   Oh, _____ sin -   ner,

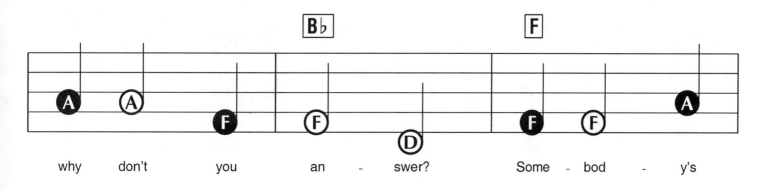

why   don't   you   an - swer?   Some - bod - y's

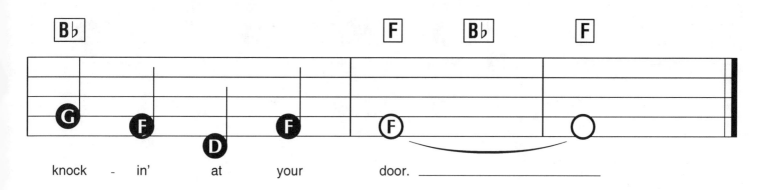

knock - in'   at   your   door. _____

Sometimes I Feel Like a Motherless Child

Registration 4
Rhythm: Ballad or Fox Trot

African-American Spiritual

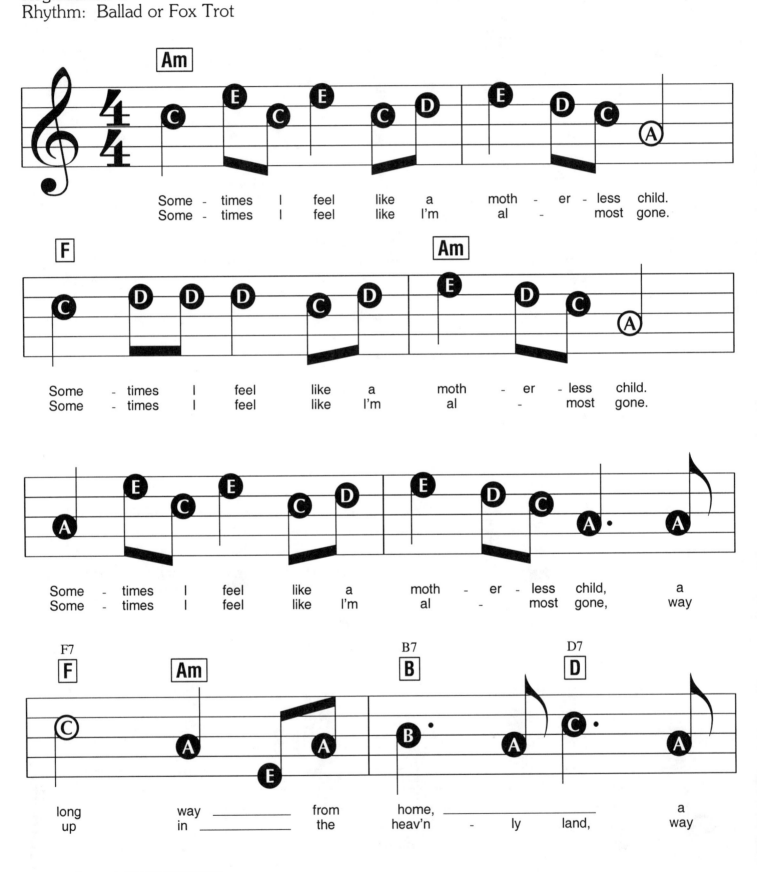

107

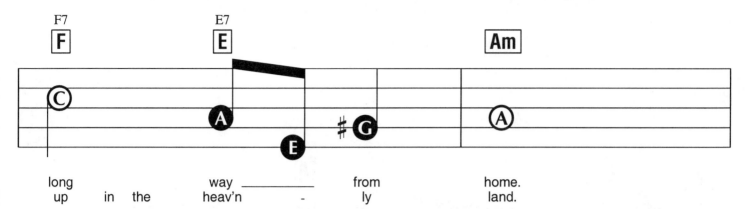

long way from home.
up in the heav'n - ly land.

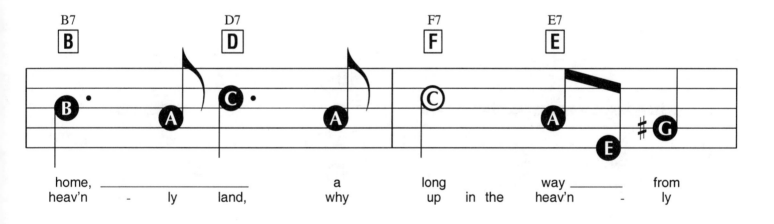

(True be - liev - er.) A long way from
(True be - liev - er.) Way up in the

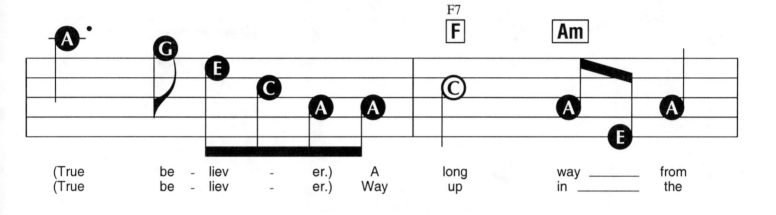

home, a long way from
heav'n - ly land, why up in the heav'n - ly

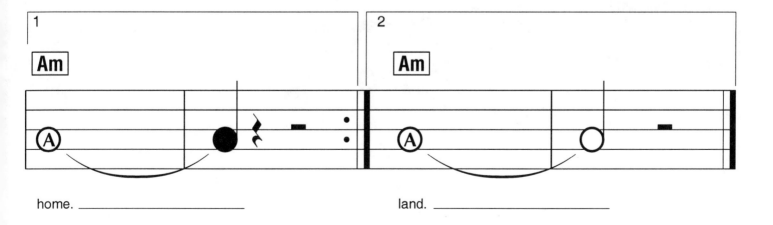

home. land.

Soon Ah Will Be Done

Registration 2
Rhythm: Swing

African-American Spiritual

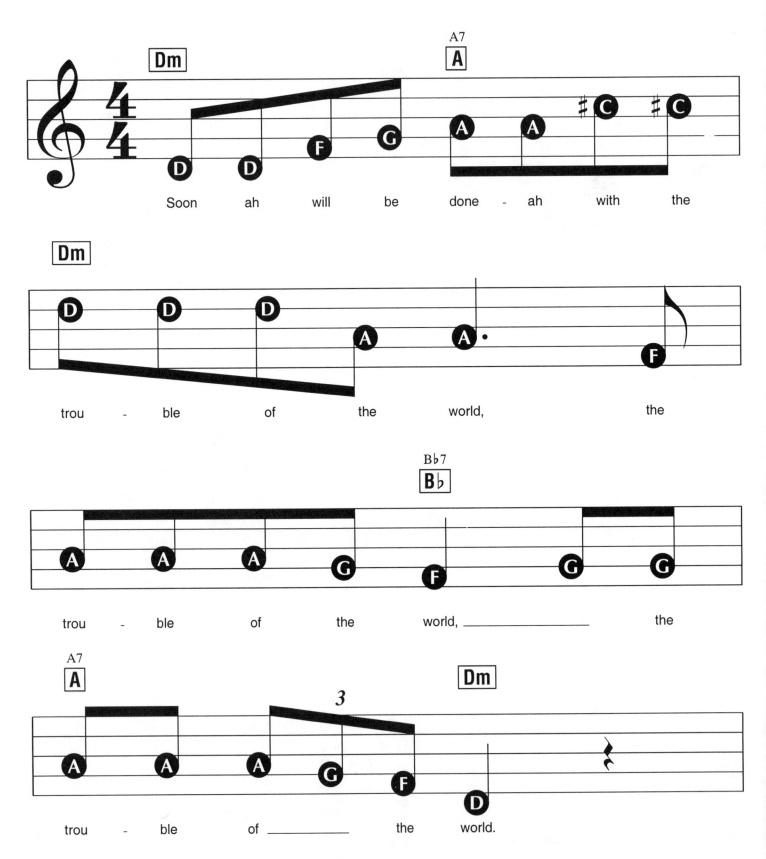

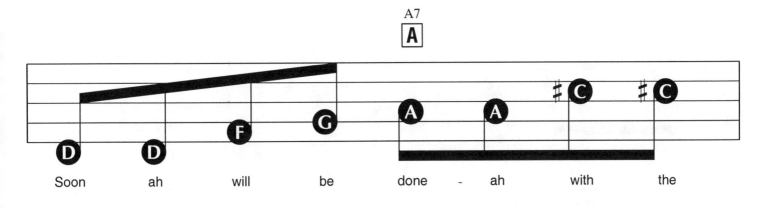

Soon ah will be done - ah with the

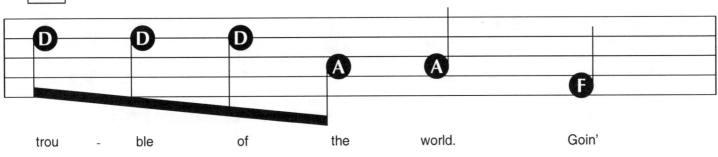

trou - ble of the world. Goin'

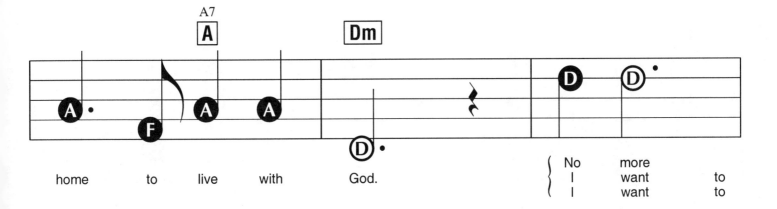

home to live with God.

No more I want to
I want to

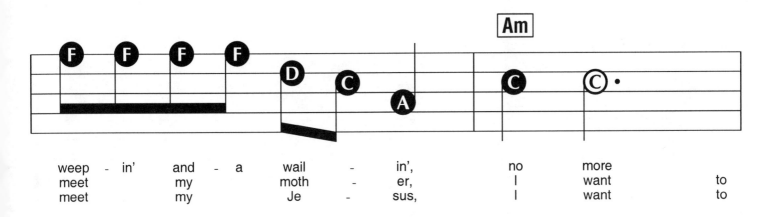

weep - in' and - a wail - in', no more
meet my moth - er, I want to
meet my Je - sus, I want to

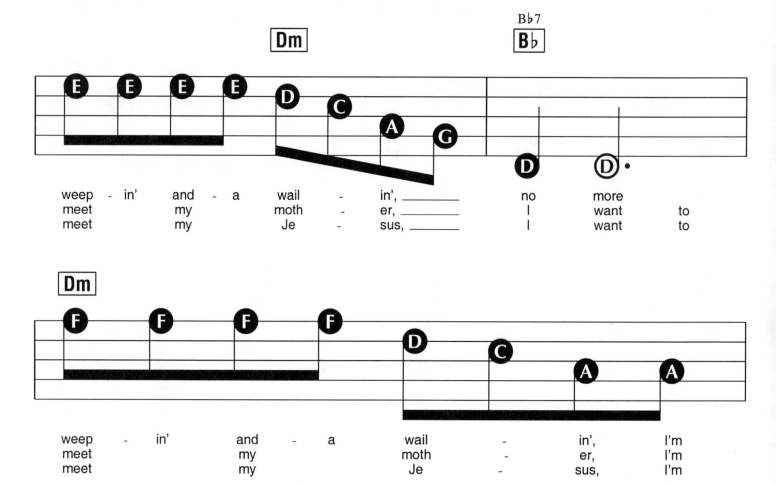

weep - in' and - a wail - in', _____ no more
meet my moth - er, _____ I want to
meet my Je - sus, _____ I want to

weep - in' and - a wail - in', I'm
meet my moth - er, I'm
meet my Je - sus, I'm

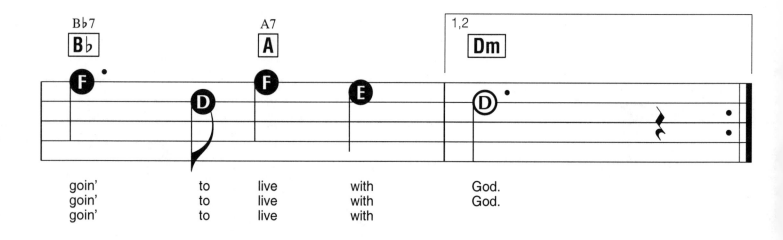

goin' to live with God.
goin' to live with God.
goin' to live with

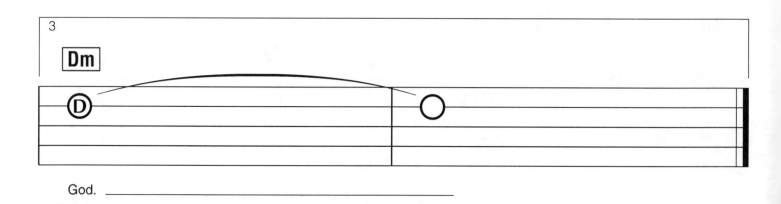

God. _____

Standin' in the Need of Prayer

Registration 2
Rhythm: Swing

African-American Spiritual

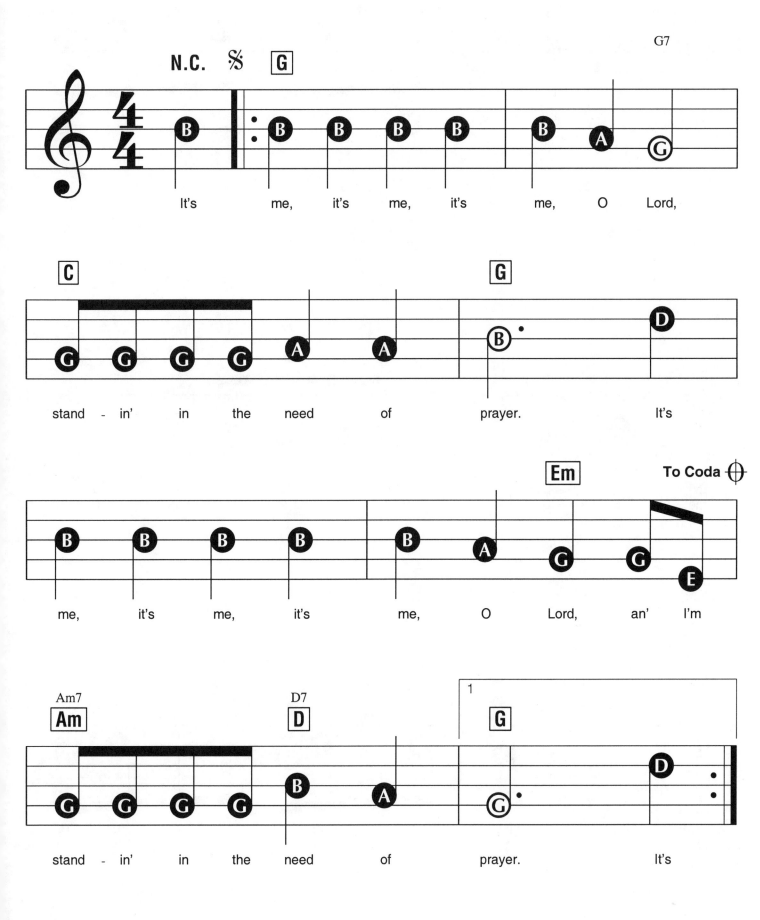

112

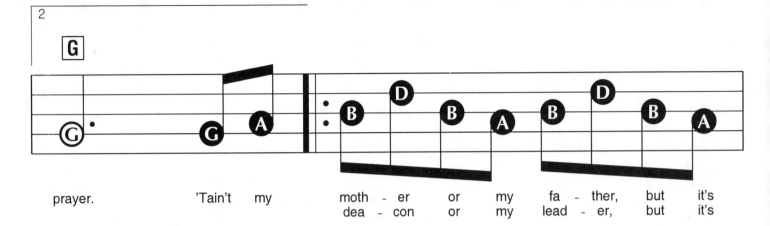

prayer.   'Tain't my   moth - er or my fa - ther, but it's
                       dea - con or my lead - er, but it's

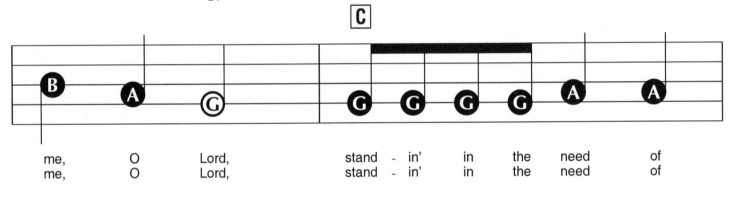

me, O Lord, stand - in' in the need of
me, O Lord, stand - in' in the need of

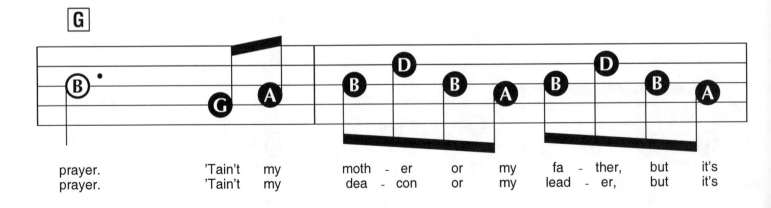

prayer.   'Tain't my   moth - er or my fa - ther, but it's
prayer.   'Tain't my   dea - con or my lead - er, but it's

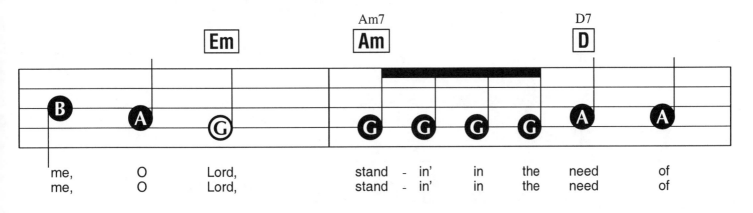

me, O Lord, stand - in' in the need of
me, O Lord, stand - in' in the need of

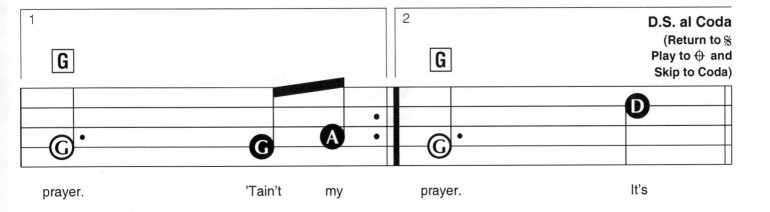

prayer. 'Tain't my prayer. It's

D.S. al Coda
(Return to 𝄋
Play to ⊕ and
Skip to Coda)

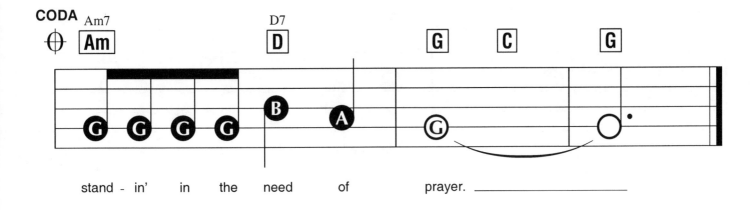

stand - in' in the need of prayer.

Sourwood Mountain

Registration 4
Rhythm: Country or Fox Trot

Southern Appalachian Folksong

Chick - ens a - crow - in' on Sour - wood Moun - tain,
I call my dar - ling a blue - eyed dai - sy,
Ducks go a - swim - ming a - cross the riv - er,

Hey! Hey! Dee - dee um day.

So man - y pret - ty girls I can't count 'em,
If she won't have me, I'll sure go cra - zy,
And in the win - ter we sure do shiv - er,

Hey! Hey! Dee - dee um day.

115

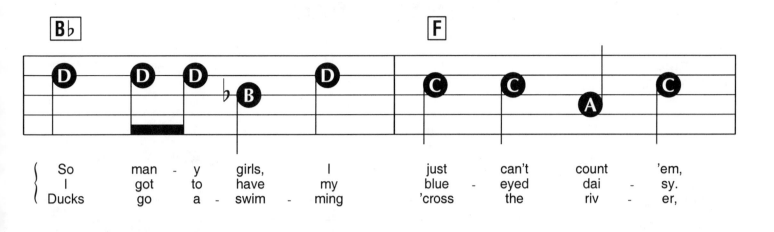

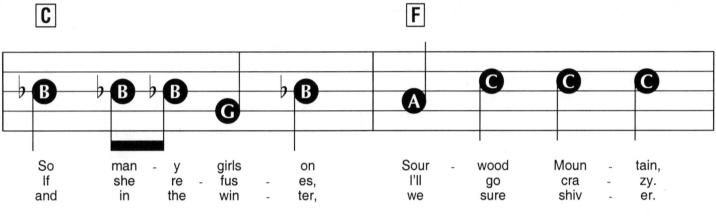

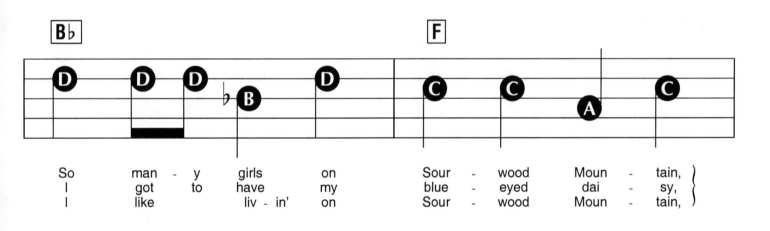

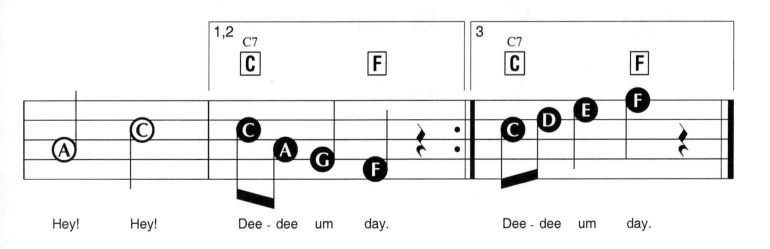

Steal Away

Registration 3
Rhythm: Pops

African-American Spiritual

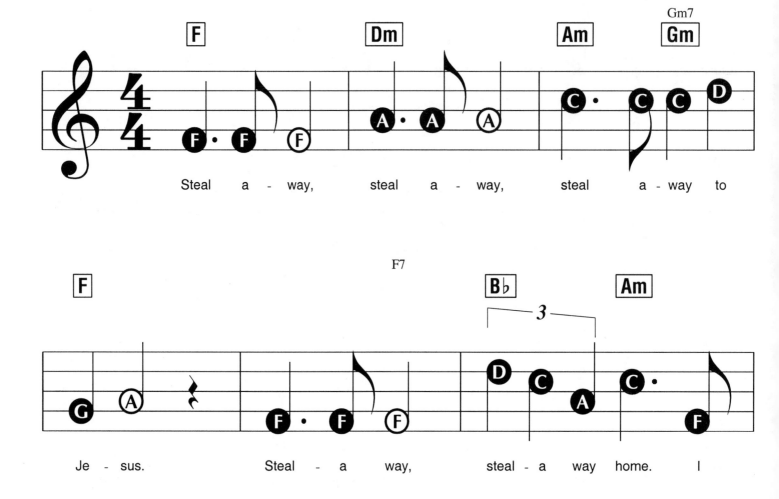

Steal a - way, steal a - way, steal a - way to

Je - sus. Steal - a way, steal - a way home. I

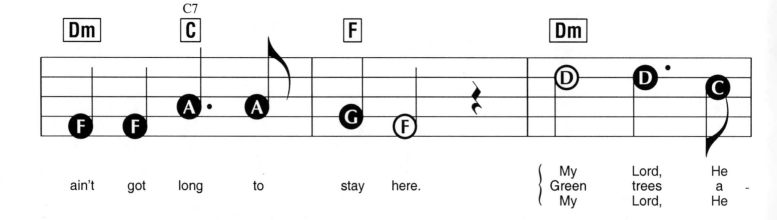

ain't got long to stay here.

My Lord, He
Green trees a -
My Lord, He

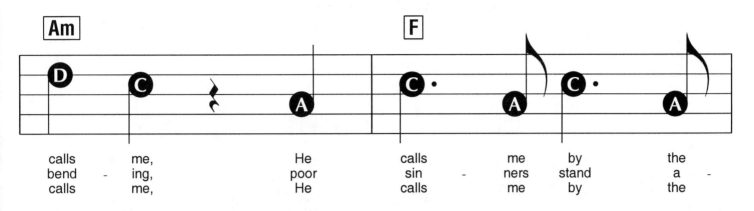

calls   me,   He   calls   me   by   the
bend - ing,   poor   sin - ners stand   a -
calls   me,   He   calls   me   by   the

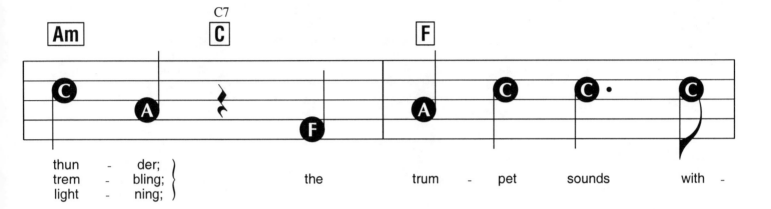

thun - der;   the   trum - pet   sounds   with -
trem - bling;
light - ning;

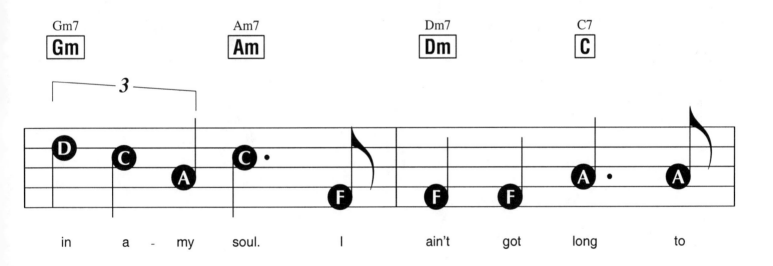

in   a - my   soul.   I   ain't   got   long   to

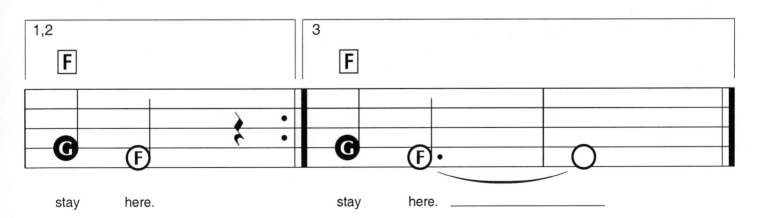

stay   here.   stay   here. _____

Streets of Laredo

Registration 3
Rhythm: Waltz

American Cowboy Song

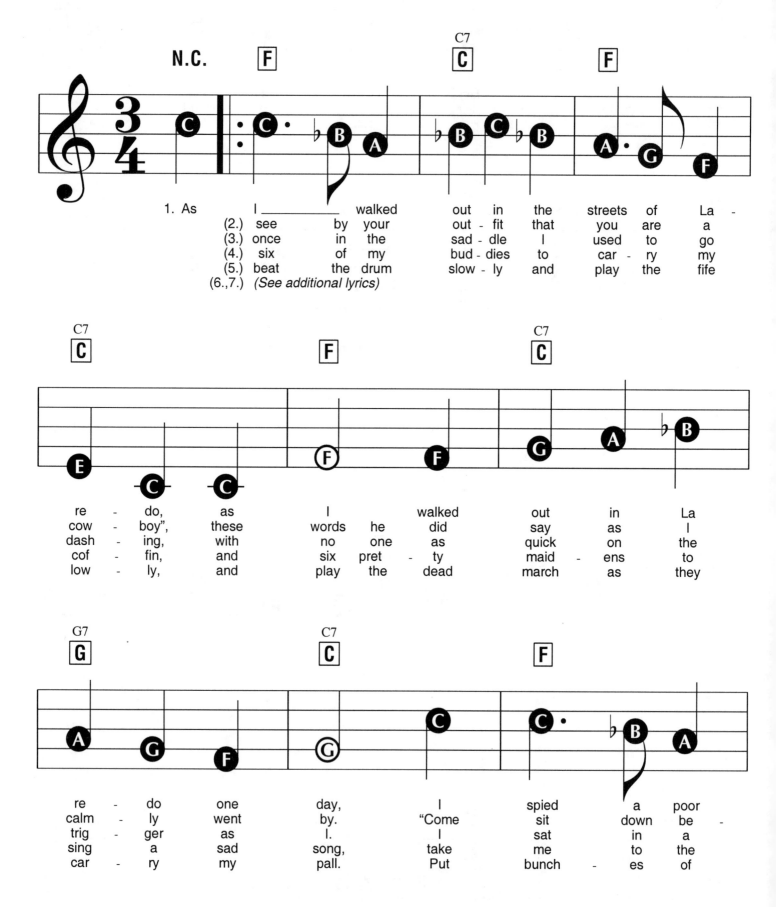

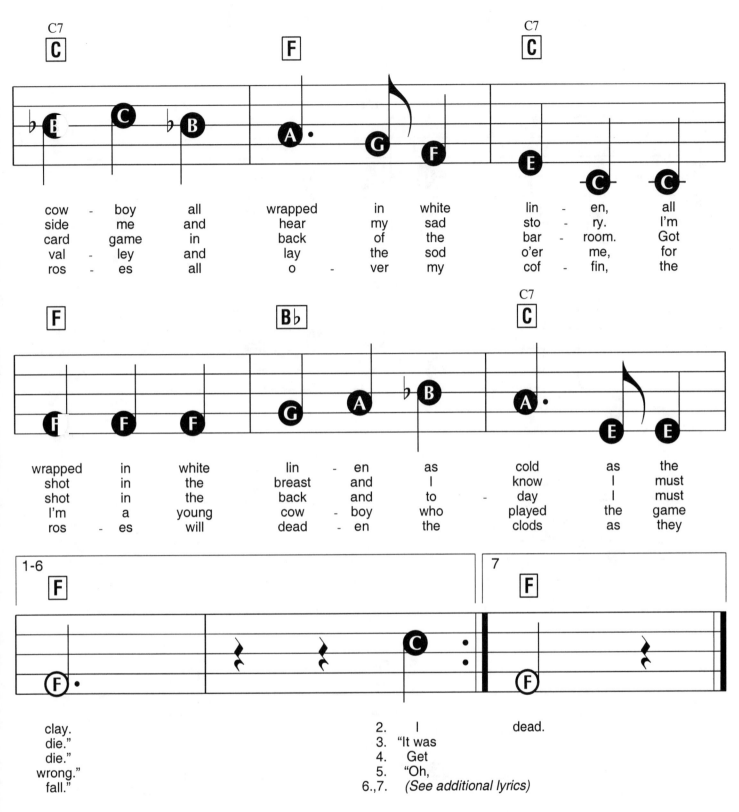

cow - boy all wrapped in white lin - en, all
side me and hear my sad sto - ry. I'm
card game in back of the bar - room. Got
val - ley and lay the sod o'er me, for
ros - es all o - ver my cof - fin, the

wrapped in white lin - en as cold as the
shot in the breast and I know I must
shot in the back and to - day I must
I'm a young cow - boy who played the game
ros - es will dead - en the clods as they

1-6 F | **7** F

clay.
die."
die."
wrong."
fall."

2. I dead.
3. "It was
4. Get
5. "Oh,
6.,7. *(See additional lyrics)*

Additional Lyrics

6. "Go gather around you a crowd of young cowboys,
And tell them the story of this my sad fate.
Tell one and the other before they go further,
To stop their wild roving before it's too late."

7. "Go fetch me a cup, just a cup of cold water,
To cool my parched lips," the cowboy then said.
Before I returned, his brave spirit had left him,
And, gone to his Maker, the cowboy was dead.

Sweet Betsy from Pike

Registration 5
Rhythm: Waltz

American Folksong

Turkey in the Straw

Registration 3
Rhythm: Fox Trot or Polka

American Folksong

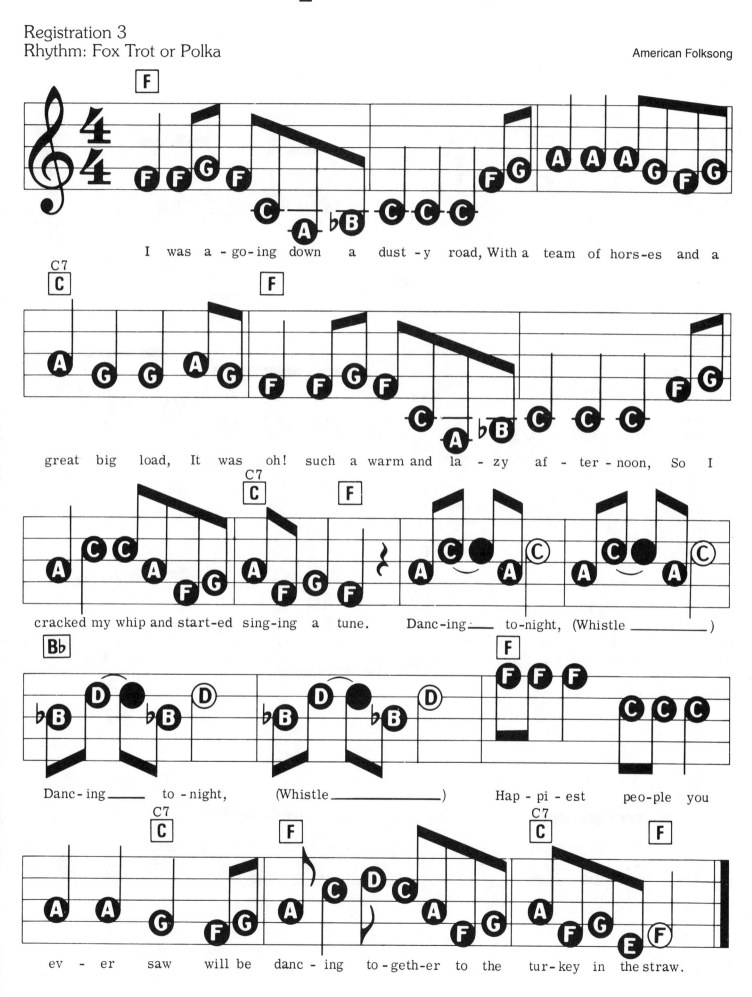

Swing Low, Sweet Chariot

Registration 4
Rhythm: Swing

Traditional Spiritual

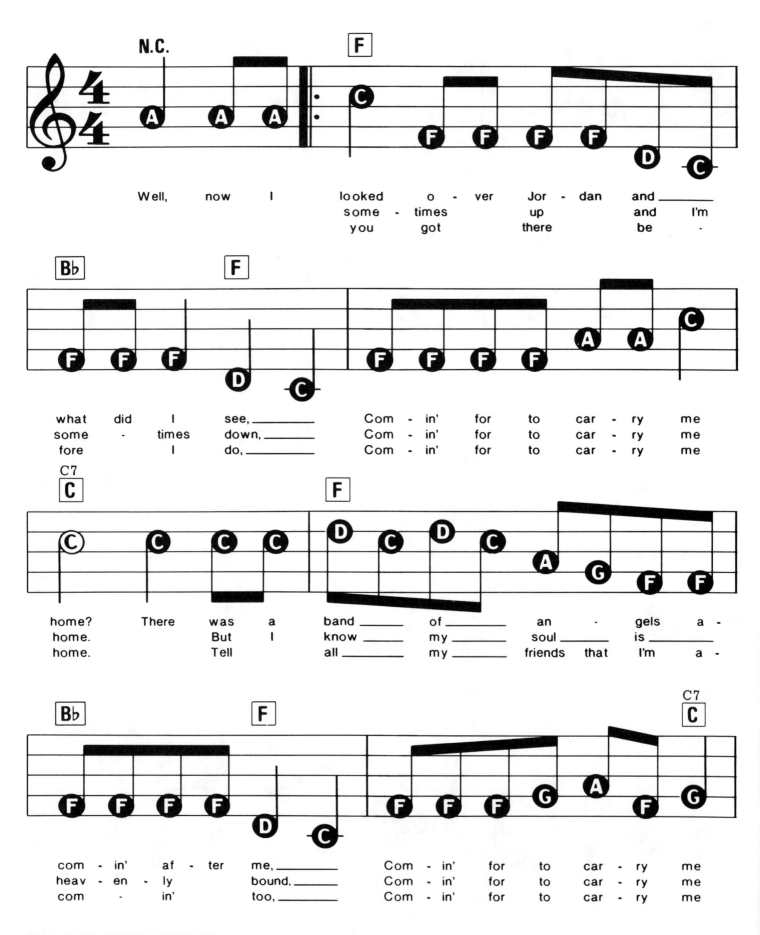

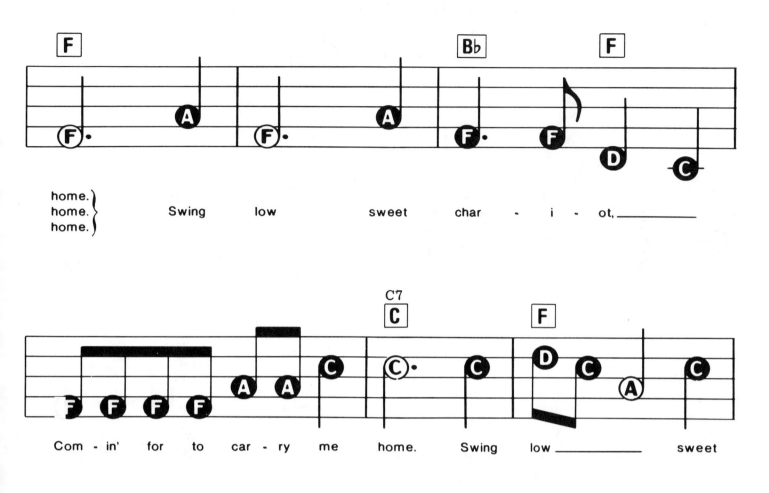

home.
home.
home.
Swing   low   sweet   char - i - ot,_____

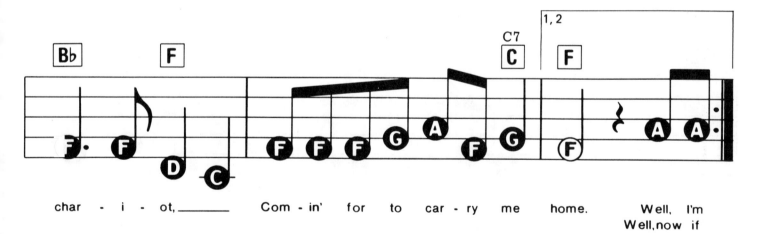

Com - in' for to car - ry me home.   Swing low_____ sweet

Bb   F

char - i - ot,____ Com - in' for to car - ry me home.   Well, I'm
                                                                Well, now if

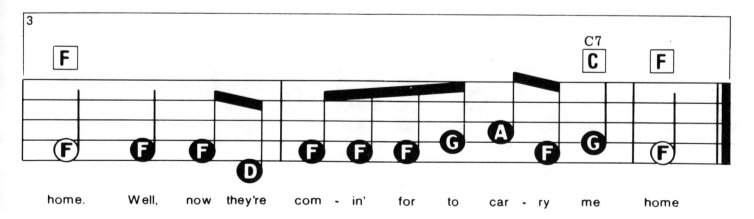

home. Well, now they're com - in' for to car - ry me home

There Is a Balm in Gilead

Registration 3
Rhythm: Pops

African-American Spiritual

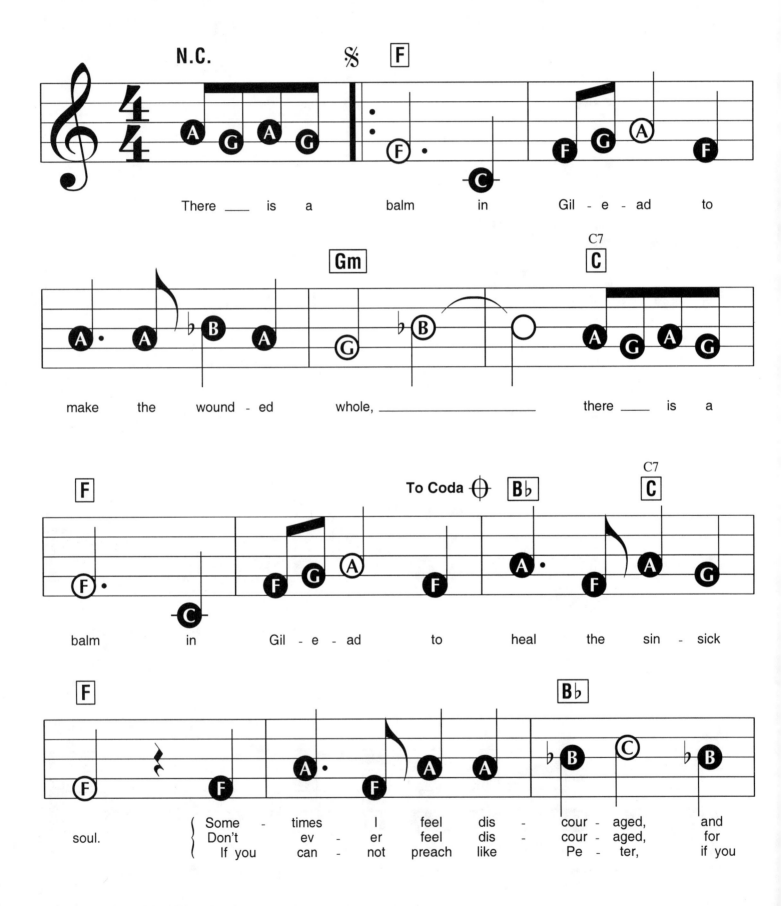

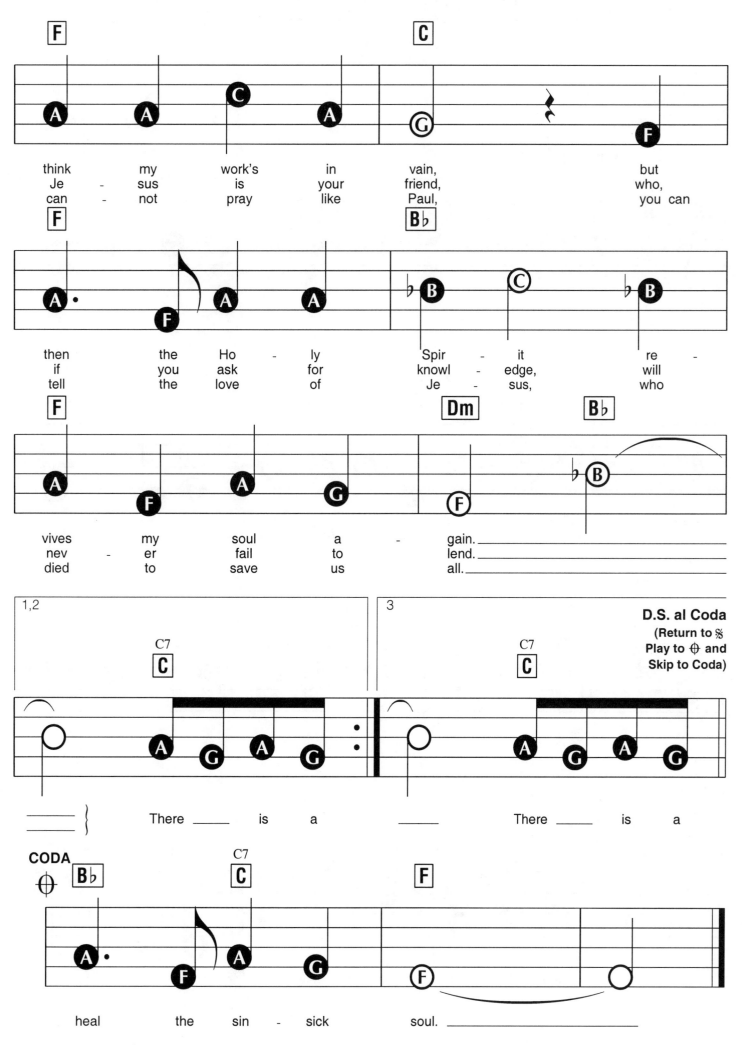

There Is a Tavern in the Town

Registration 8
Rhythm: Swing

Traditional Drinking Song

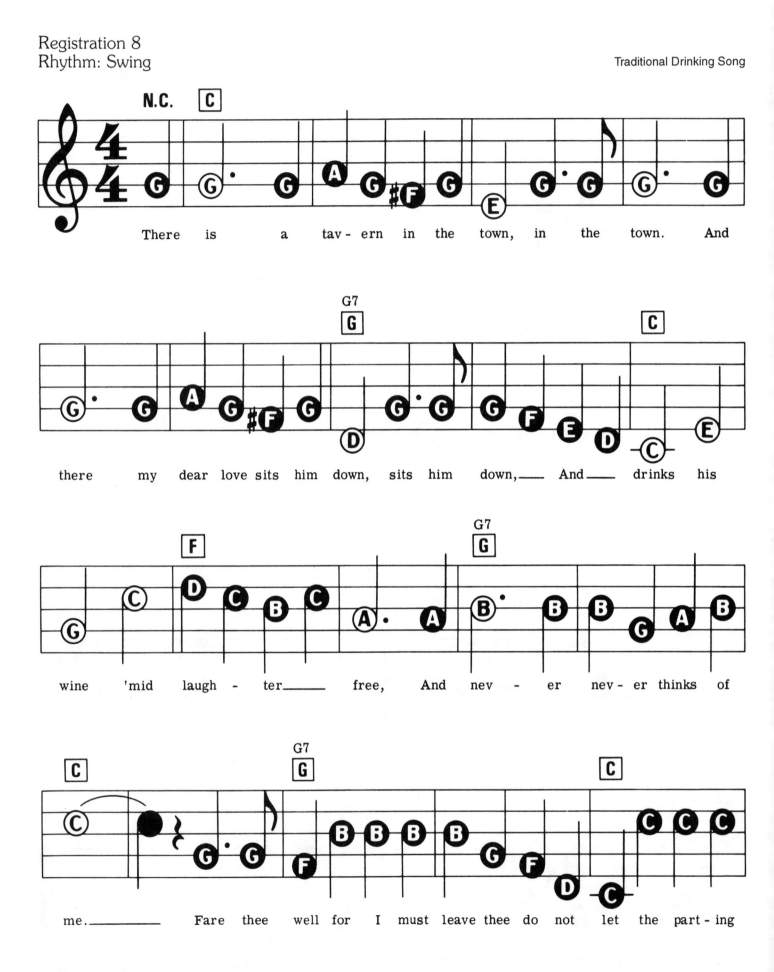

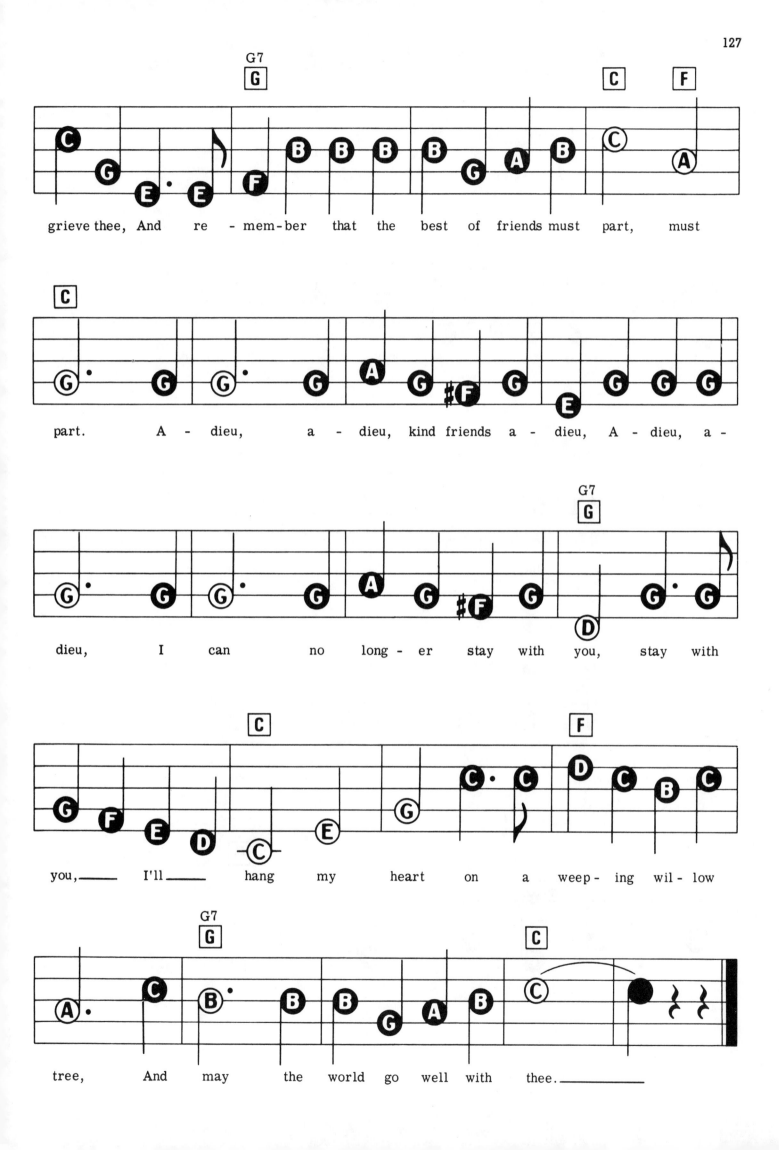

This Little Light of Mine

Registration 4
Rhythm: Fox Trot or Swing

African-American Spiritual

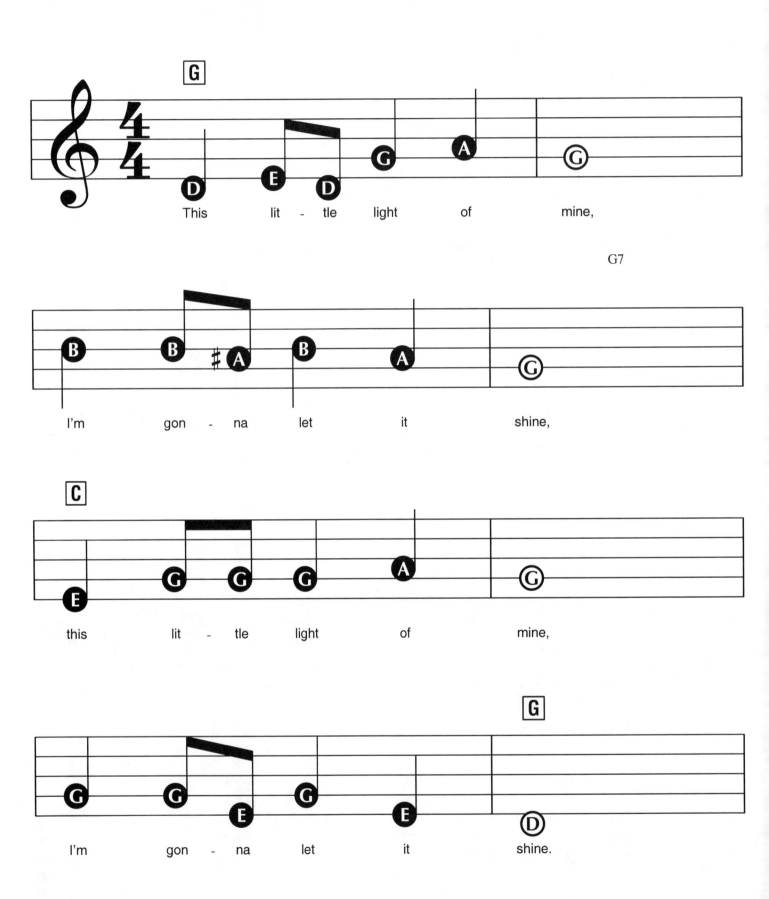

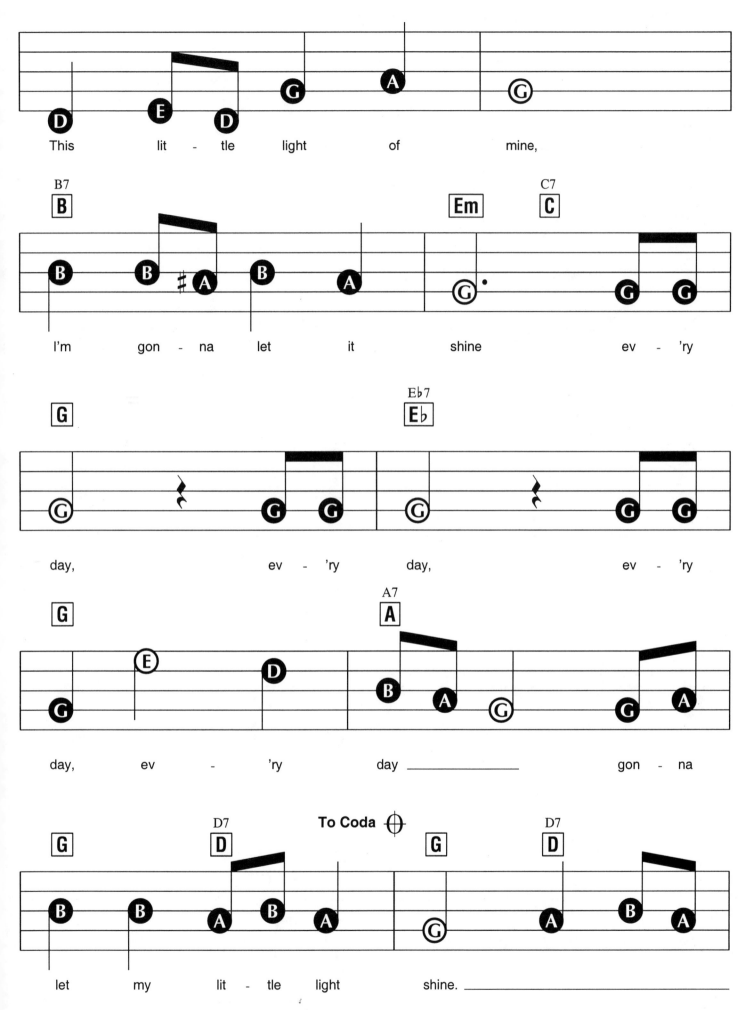

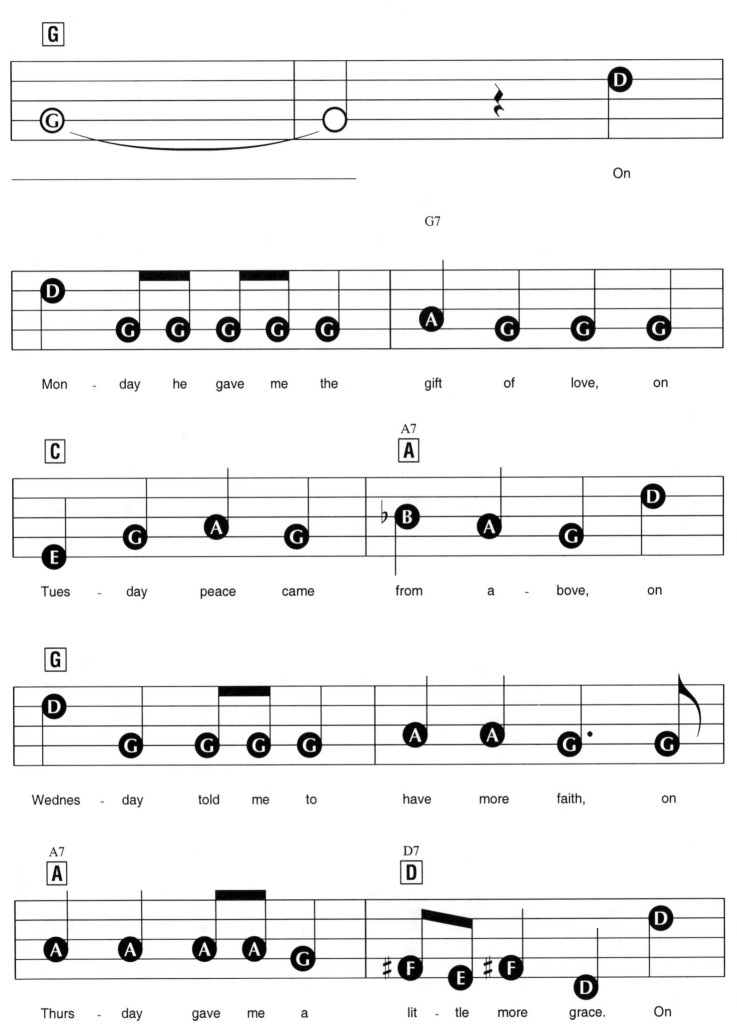

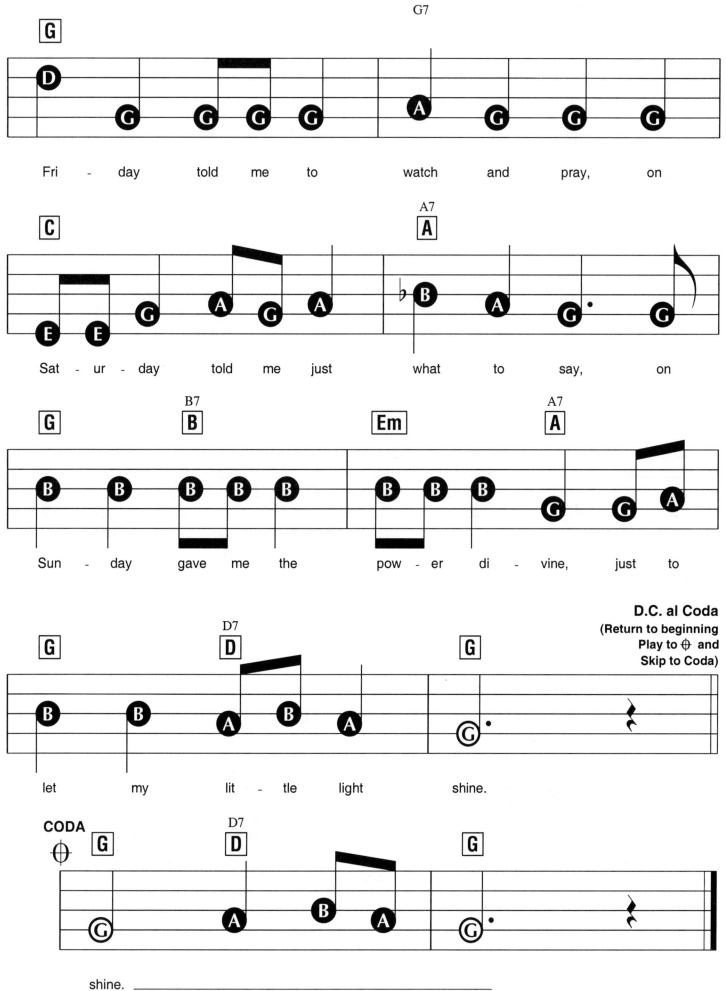

The Wabash Cannon Ball

Registration 8
Rhythm: Country or Fox Trot

Hobo Song

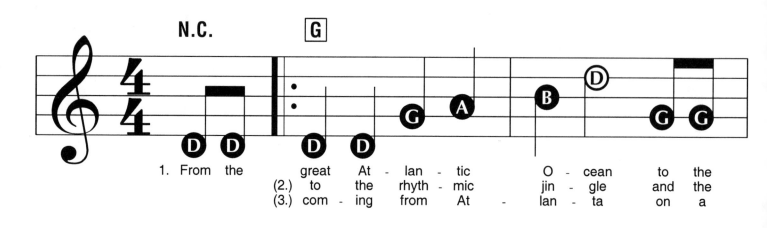

1. From the great At - lan - tic O - cean to the
(2.) to the rhyth - mic jin - gle and the
(3.) com - ing from At - lan - ta on a

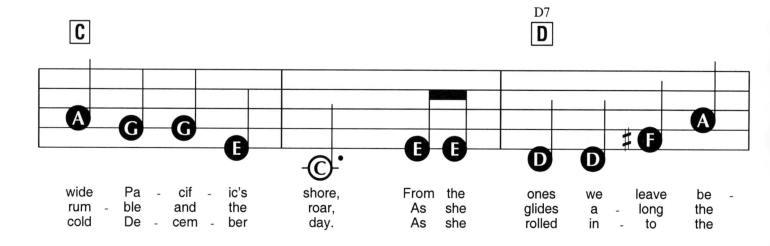

wide Pa - cif - ic's shore, From the ones we leave be -
rum - ble and the roar, As she glides a - long the
cold De - cem - ber day. As she rolled in - to the

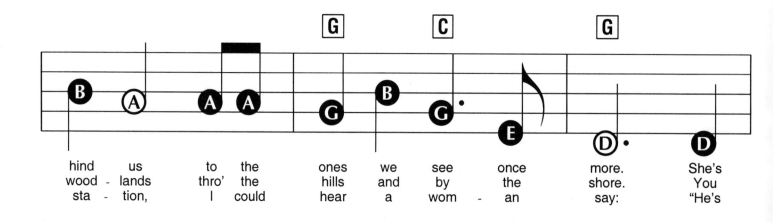

hind us to the ones we see once more. She's
wood - lands thro' the hills and by the shore. You
sta - tion, I could hear a wom - an say: "He's

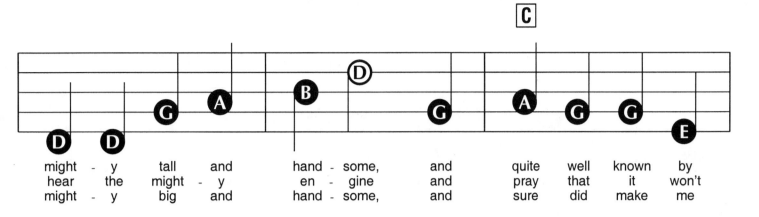

might - y   tall   and   hand - some,   and   quite   well   known   by
hear   the   might - y   en - gine   and   pray   that   it   won't
might - y   big   and   hand - some,   and   sure   did   make   me

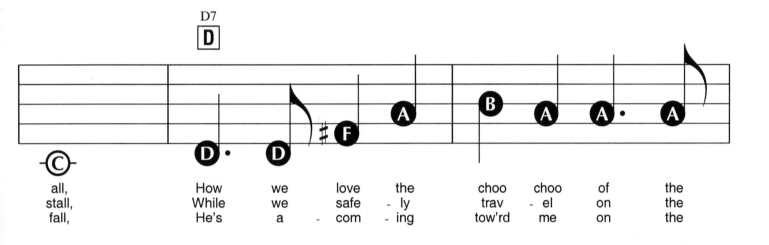

all,   How   we   love   the   choo   choo   of   the
stall,   While   we   safe - ly   trav - el   on   the
fall,   He's   a - com - ing   tow'rd   me   on   the

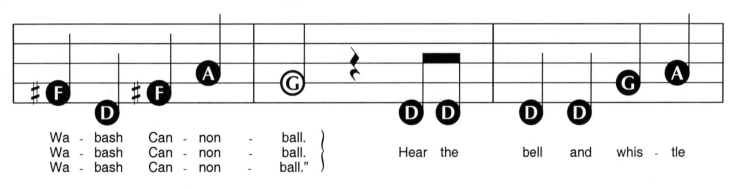

Wa - bash   Can - non - ball.
Wa - bash   Can - non - ball.
Wa - bash   Can - non - ball."

Hear   the   bell   and   whis - tle

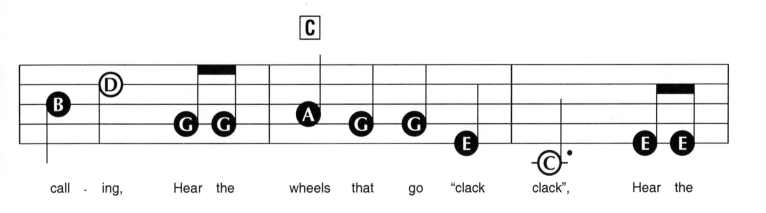

call - ing,   Hear   the   wheels   that   go   "clack   clack",   Hear   the

134

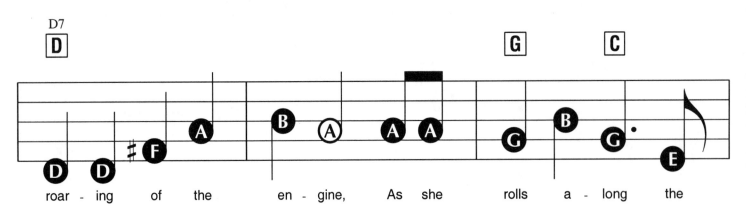

roar - ing of the en - gine, As she rolls a - long the

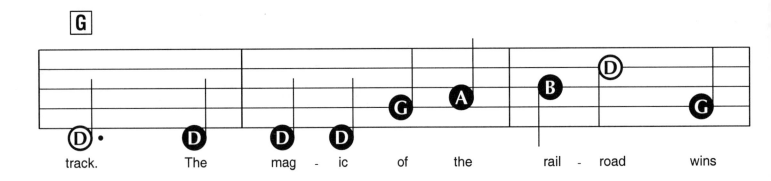

track. The mag - ic of the rail - road wins

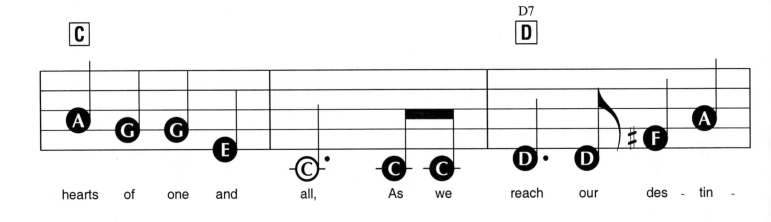

hearts of one and all, As we reach our des - tin -

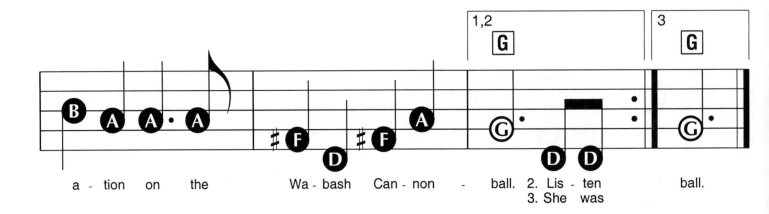

a - tion on the Wa - bash Can - non - ball. 2. Lis - ten   ball.
3. She was

When the Saints Go Marching In

Registration 2
Rhythm: March or Swing

Words by Katherine E. Purvis
Music by James M. Black

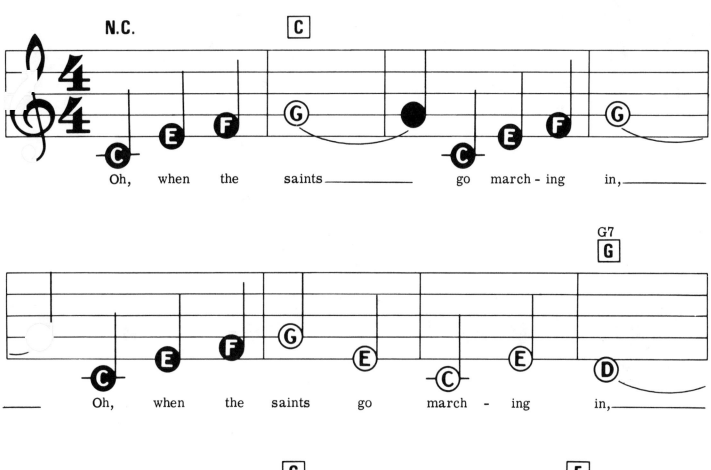

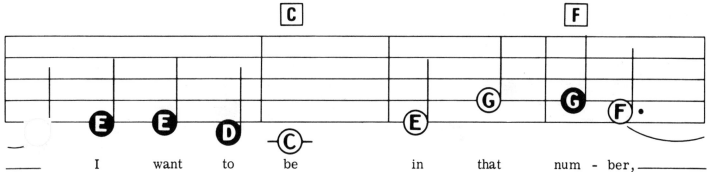

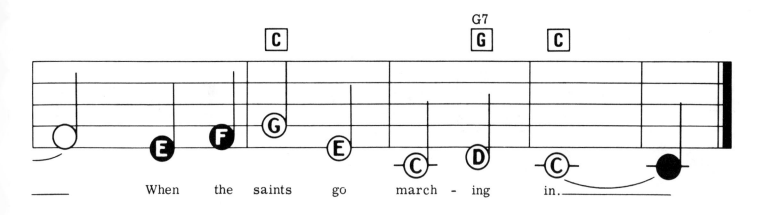

Wayfaring Stranger

Registration 8
Rhythm: Swing

Southern American Folk Hymn

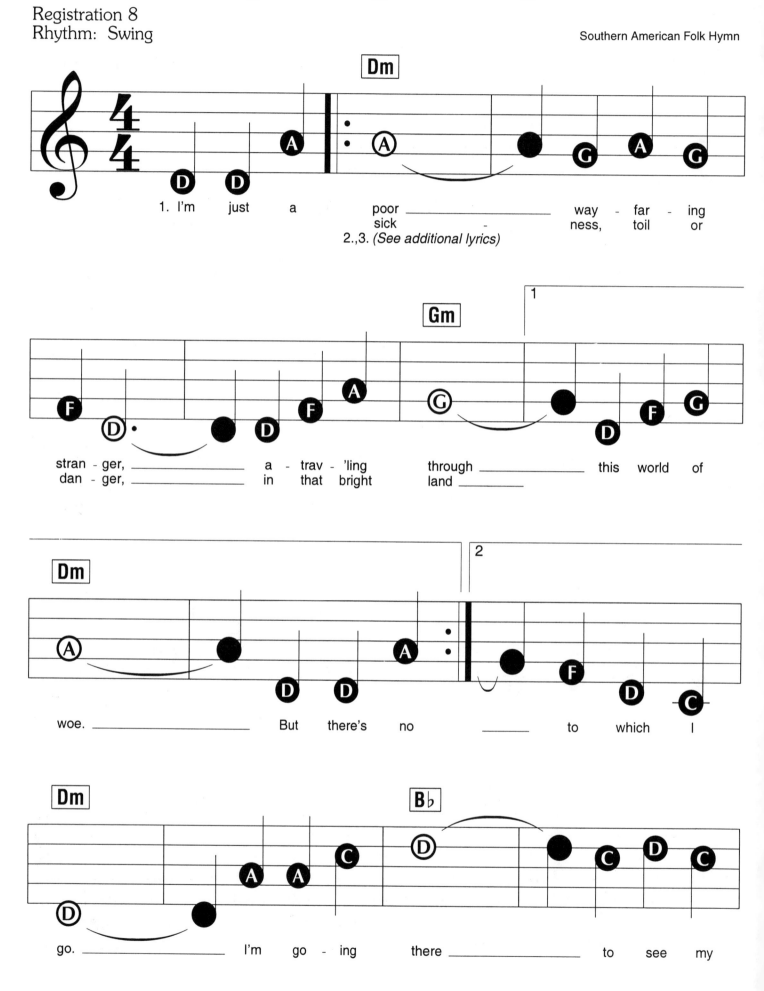

1. I'm just a poor _____ way - far - ing
sick - ness, toil or
2.,3. *(See additional lyrics)*

stran - ger, _____ a - trav - 'ling through _____ this world of
dan - ger, _____ in that bright land _____

woe. _____ But there's no _____ to which I

go. _____ I'm go - ing there _____ to see my

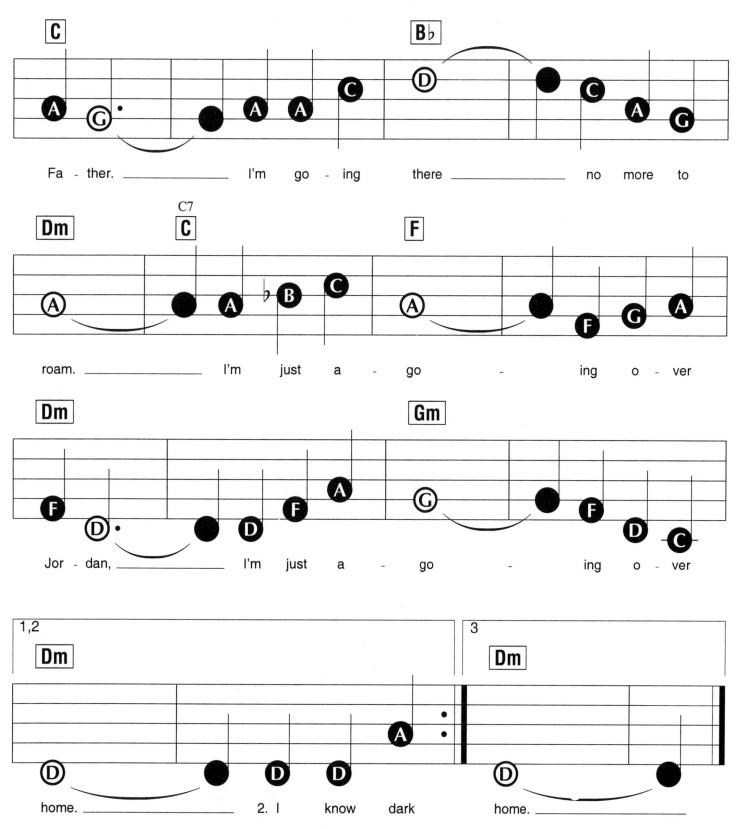

Additional Lyrics

2. I know dark clouds will gather 'round me,
I know my way is steep and rough.
But beauteous fields lie just beyond me
Where souls redeemed their vigil keep.
I'm going there to meet my mother,
She said she'd meet me when I come...

3. I want to wear a crown of glory
When I get home to that bright land.
I want to shout Salvation's story,
In concert with that bloodwashed band.
I'm going there to meet my Saviour,
To sing His praise forever more...

When Johnny Comes Marching Home

Registration 4
Rhythm: 6/8 March

Words and Music by
Patrick Sarsfield Gilmore

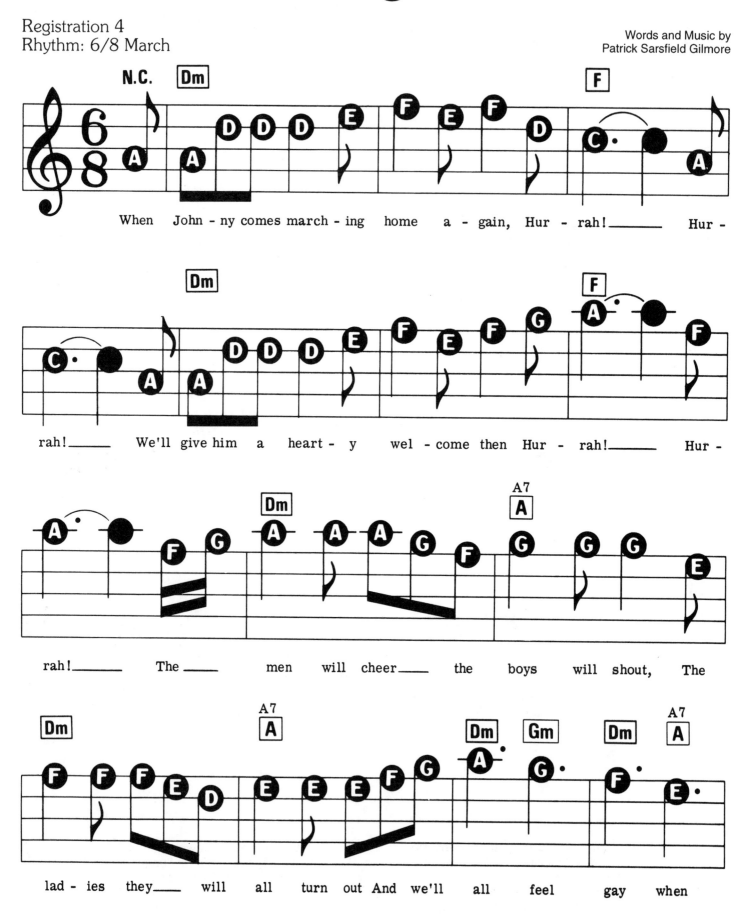

When John - ny comes march - ing home a - gain, Hur - rah!_____ Hur -

rah!_____ We'll give him a heart - y wel - come then Hur - rah!_____ Hur -

rah!_____ The _____ men will cheer_____ the boys will shout, The

lad - ies they_____ will all turn out And we'll all feel gay when

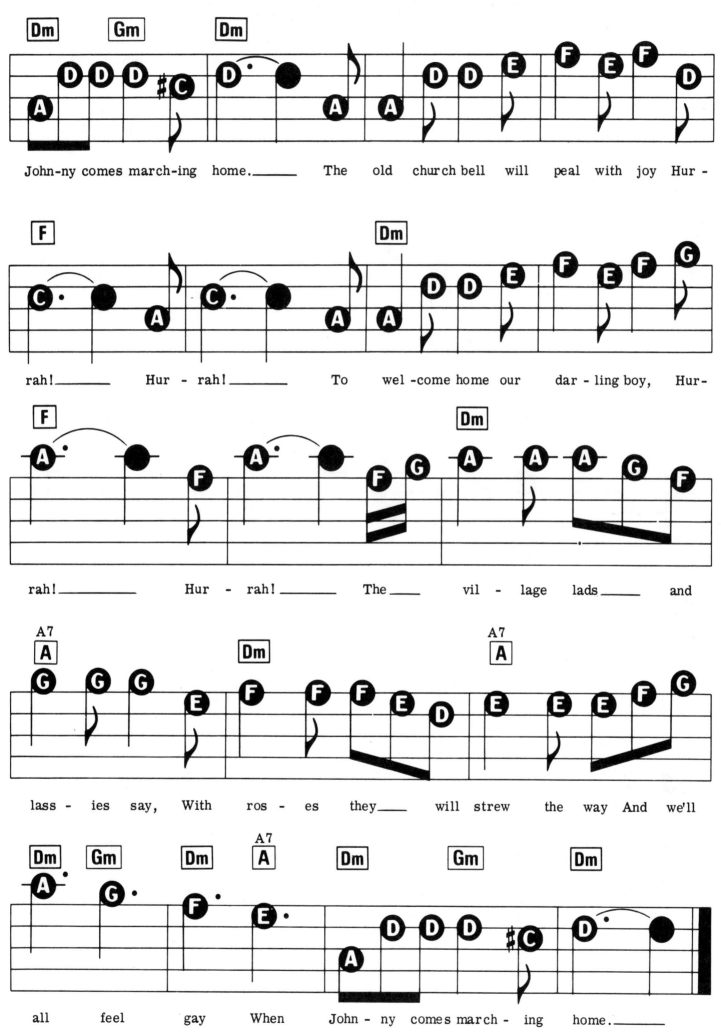

Wondrous Love

Registration 9
Rhythm: Fox Trot

Southern American Folk Hymn

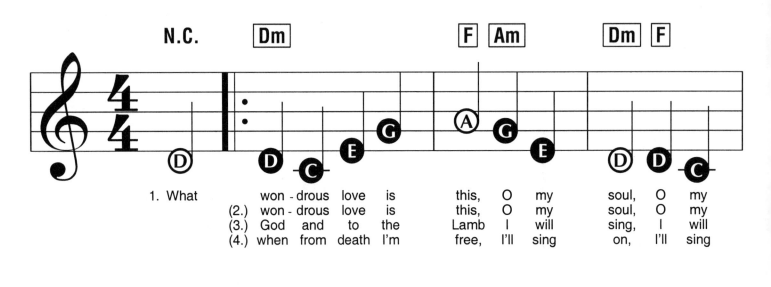

1. What	won-drous love is	this, O my	soul, O my	
(2.)	won-drous love is	this, O my	soul, O my	
(3.)	God and to the	Lamb I will	sing, I will	
(4.)	when from death I'm	free, I'll sing	on, I'll sing	

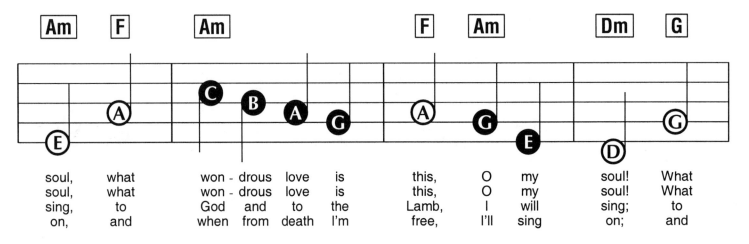

soul,	what	won-drous love is	this, O my	soul! What
soul,	what	won-drous love is	this, O my	soul! What
sing,	to	God and to the	Lamb, I will	sing; to
on,	and	when from death I'm	free, I'll sing	on; and

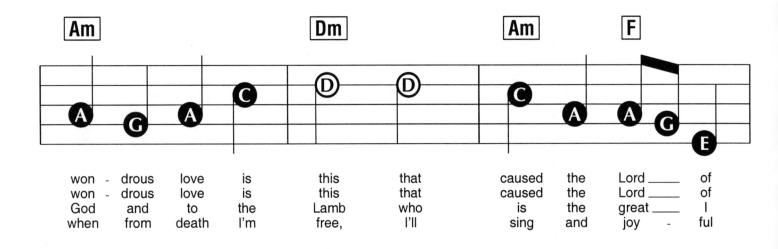

won-drous love is	this	that	caused the Lord ___ of
won-drous love is	this	that	caused the Lord ___ of
God and to the	Lamb	who	is the great ___ I
when from death I'm	free,	I'll	sing and joy - ful

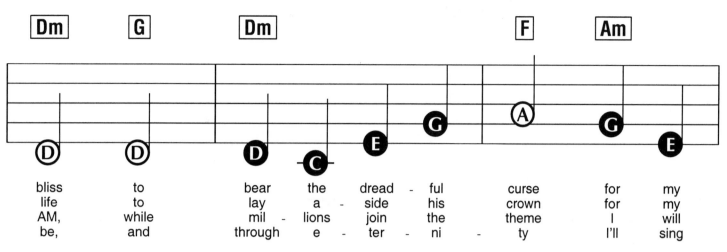

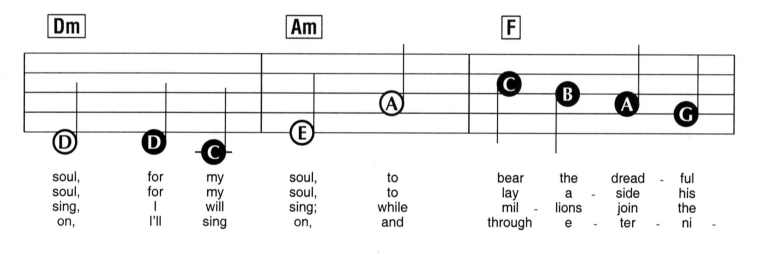

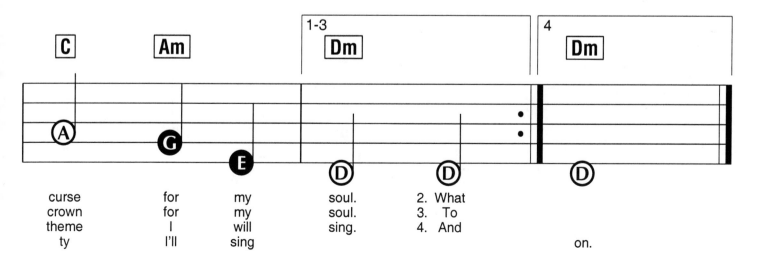

Yankee Doodle

Registration 9
Rhythm: March

Traditional

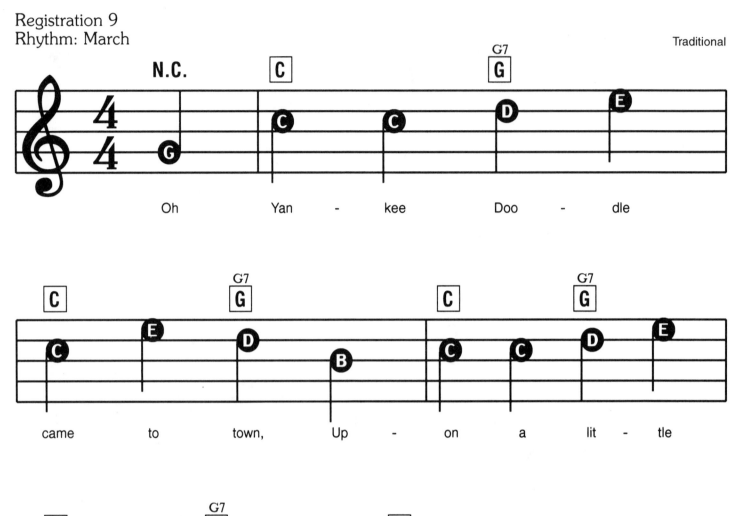

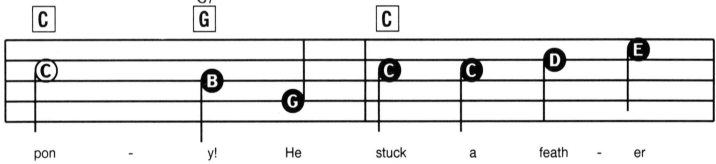

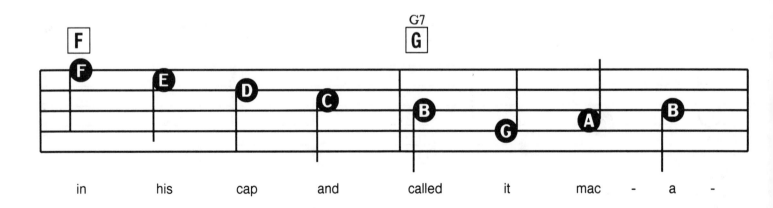

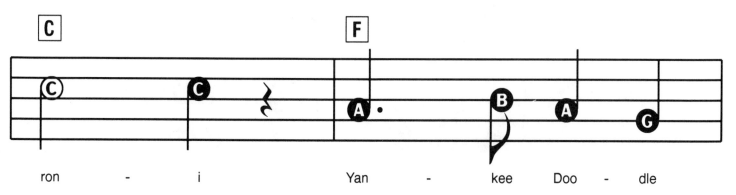

ron - i Yan - kee Doo - dle

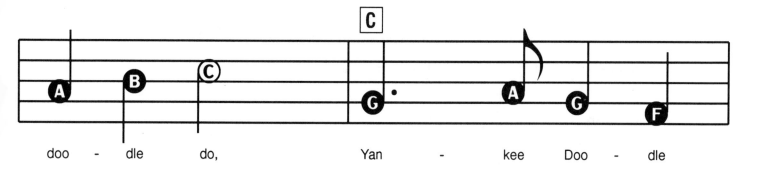

doo - dle do, Yan - kee Doo - dle

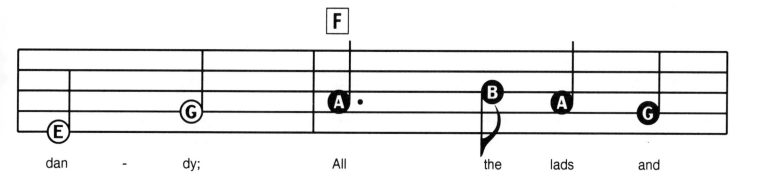

dan - dy; All the lads and

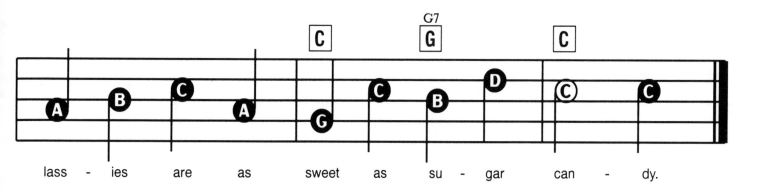

lass - ies are as sweet as su - gar can - dy.

Registration Guide

• Match the Registration number on the song to the corresponding numbered category below. Select and activate an instrumental sound available on your instrument.

• Choose an automatic rhythm appropriate to the mood and style of the song. (Consult your Owner's Guide for proper operation of automatic rhythm features.)

• Adjust the tempo and volume controls to comfortable settings.

Registration

1	Mellow	Flutes, Clarinet, Oboe, Flugel Horn, Trombone, French Horn, Organ Flutes
2	Bright	Saxophones, Trumpet, Mute Trumpet, Synth Leads, Jazz/Gospel Organs
3	Guitars	Acoustic/Electric Guitars, Banjo, Mandolin, Dulcimer, Ukulele, Hawaiian Guitar
4	Strings	Violin, Viola, Cello, Fiddle, String Ensemble, Pizzicato, Organ Strings
5	Mallets	Vibraphone, Marimba, Xylophone, Steel Drums, Bells, Celesta, Chimes
6	Bellows	Accordion, French Accordion, Mussette, Harmonica, Pump Organ, Bagpipes
7	Liturgical	Pipe Organ, Hand Bells, Vocal Ensemble, Choir, Organ Flutes
8	Piano	Piano, Electric Piano, Honky Tonk Piano, Harpsichord, Clavi
9	Novelty	Melodic Percussion, Wah Trumpet, Synth, Whistle, Kazoo, Perc. Organ
10	Ensemble	Brass Section, Sax Section, Wind Ensemble, Full Organ, Theater Organ